695

FISCHBACH LIBR
PEOPLES CHU
EAST LANSING, MICHIGAN

P9-CCC-225

Nurtu

CHOICES

GUIDES FOR TODAY'S WOMAN

Nurture

Elaine Donelson

The Westminster Press
Philadelphia

Copyright © 1984 Elaine Donelson

All rights reserved—no part of this book may be reproduced in any form without permission in writing from the publisher, except by a reviewer who wishes to quote brief passages in connection with a review in magazine or newspaper.

Book Design by Alice Derr

First edition

Published by The Westminster Press®
Philadelphia, Pennsylvania

PRINTED IN THE UNITED STATES OF AMERICA
9 8 7 6 5 4 3 2 1

Library of Congress Cataloging in Publication Data

Donelson, Elaine.
  Nurture.

  (Choices : guides for today's woman)
  Bibliography: p.
  1. Helping behavior. 2. Love. 3. Friendship.
4. Women—Psychology. 5. Women—Social conditions.
I. Title. II. Series: Choices.
BF637.H4D66 1984   158'.2   83-25906
ISBN 0-664-24546-3 (pbk.)

158.2
D

FISCHBACH LIBRARY
PEOPLES CHURCH
EAST LANSING, MICHIGAN

To those who have taught me about Nurture, by walking
beside me, leading me, and following me in the struggle
to be human, especially,

> My psychological and biological parents,
> LOU and FRED

> My psychological sister,
> DONNA

They have journeyed into the Valley of the Shadows,
And returned to the Green Pastures of Shepherding care,
to love and to be loved.

On the day I called, you answered me, my strength of
soul you increased.   (Psalm 138:3)

Two are better than one, because they have a good
reward for their toil. For if they fall, one will lift up the
other.   (Ecclesiastes 4:9–10)

CONTENTS

PUBLISHER'S ACKNOWLEDGMENT

The publisher gratefully acknowledges the advice of several distinguished scholars in planning this series. Virginia Mollenkott, Arlene Swidler, Phyllis Trible, and Ann Ulanov helped shape the goals of the series, identify vital topics, and locate knowledgeable authors. Views expressed in the books, of course, are those of the individual writers and not of the advisers.

CHAPTER 1

Nurture:
Giving and Receiving
in Personal Growth

"Sometimes I feel so inadequate—I want to give to people, and I feel really good when I do. But there are times when nothing works right."

"Sometimes I feel guilty. I want someone to give something to me! I don't think I'm a selfish person. But there comes a point, and I really feel selfish . . . and then guilty."

"Sometimes it seems like I have a right to *be* only if I'm doing something for someone else. That doesn't seem right, but it seems like it is that way."

"Sometimes I feel so alone. . . . I know I'm not, really, but I feel alone."

Many people have such thoughts, and some have them without being able to express them, even to close friends or other loved ones. The feelings are likely to be normal. Being a good person, particularly a woman person, is said to mean giving to other people. And we try! When we do not feel successful or do not think we can keep on trying to give, we conclude: "Something must be wrong with me!" Deciding that we should try harder to be more giving does not usually solve any problems.

Being a mature, healthy human being does involve

giving to others, but we are taught very little about what that means. Much effort is misspent as we rush around trying to be caring and loving people, giving, giving, giving to others. The effort could be directed better so that there is greater joy in giving and receiving. In this book, I'll offer food for thought on how we can give better to one another and to ourselves.

SCOPE AND ISSUES

GOALS

This book is about nurture, support, friendship, love, collegiality, at home or on the job. The general goal, of course, is to help improve the quantity and the quality of nurturing relationships. There are two big messages. First, nurture is not just a matter of giving to other people. It also involves receiving nurture from others, and nurturing ourselves. Loving oneself and loving others go together. Second, we must take nurture seriously and pay attention in trying to be nurturing. People often jump the gun, so to speak, and do not think carefully about why they give and about what they give. Because of bad habits, they do not give effectively or they miss opportunities for giving. Good nurture is a highly active process that requires a great deal of personal insight, knowledge, and involvement. With more thought, we can be in a better position to make good choices about what to do. This chapter gives a broad overview of some of the principles that will be developed in more detail in later chapters. I will emphasize women's perspectives and women giving to women, including themselves. Yet, important truths are human truths. An increased understanding in one relationship should have benefits in other relationships as well.

WHAT IS NURTURE?

Nurture involves going out on a rainy Saturday afternoon to help a friend do something she should have done two months ago. It is a bouquet of flowers, "Just because I thought you might like it," and finding a recipe or a memo a friend wants while you are sorting through dusty files to find something you want. Nurture means feeling good because you know something helpful to tell someone else and being disappointed when you cannot help or when your help is not wanted. It involves offering without requests, responding to requests, and refusing requests. Nurture is the hard work of paying attention to others and knowing their needs, while also paying attention to ourselves and getting our own needs met. What do all these activities and features of nurture have in common besides the name "nurture"?

Fostering Growth. To nurture is to educate and foster growth, which is much the same as helping somebody be better, more mature, and healthy. The aims of nurture are like those of education. *Education* means the development of natural powers and the shaping of character. The word *education* is from the Latin *educare*, which means "to lead out." Nurture means countering ignorance—a lack in education or knowledge, or being unacquainted and unaware.

Thus, nurturing is a *process* of educating people, or pulling out, eliciting, leading out, what is in them. We are helping in their growth. Nurturing or educating people is helping them to be what they truly are, in all the beauty that sometimes only a mother or a father or God can see. Nurture is virtually the same as love, at least effective love, or productive love, or what C. S. Lewis called divine love.

Nurture is also a personal *attitude* toward life, other people, and oneself. With an attitude of love, we can better see to the inner core of beauty and strength of a person. Love helps that inner core to show itself more and more. One of my favorite phrases is from a woman theologian, Beverly Harrison: "to love into existence." I sometimes rant and rave, "I'm going to love you into existence no matter what you do!" At those times I think my friends are not being the persons they truly are. (They also rant and rave at me for the same reason.)

DISTORTED VIEWS

Women and Children. The general cultural view of nurture has been overly narrow and distorted. It amounts to seeing nurture as relevant mainly to children, and happening mainly within the family. Thus, mothers are the primary nurturers, and fathers are the secondary nurturers. Children are the primary receivers of nurture, and others in the family are the secondary receivers. The obligation to offer nurture falls on women especially. Some women get tired of the obligations and the unreasonable demands made of them. Many, too, have a broader understanding of what nurture should be.

Adult Growth. There is a widespread view that growth is more or less completed with entry into adulthood. With nurture dominantly for children who are growing, adults are left out. Adults—grown-ups—as well as children grow, and adults can use nurture in their growth, just as children can. It is also true that there is a child within every adult. Nurture is needed throughout life. The emphasis in this book is on the many opportunities for nurture in adult interactions.

Any relationship can be nurturing and supportive. People often think first and only of family relationships, with their idea of family including only those related biologically or legally. People with this rather limited view miss many other opportunities for giving and receiving, and for growing and contributing to the growth of others. They also put quite a burden on the members of their family. It would make more sense psychologically to reverse the image and define family in terms of nurture rather than define nurture in terms of family. Thus the psychological family extends to include those people with whom a person has nurturing relationships rather than narrowing the idea of nurturing to apply only to relationships within a biological and legal family. It is a broad psychological family that can provide the setting for adult growth.

NURTURE: GROWTH, ACTIONS, AND CARE

ACTING AND CARING

The effective nurture needed for growth involves inner psychological factors and outer actions. We need to understand at both levels. Thus the inner factors of "having the right attitude," "meaning well," and "seeing with love" are relevant. However, some people never get around to doing anything, because they get so concerned about sincerity, or what the moral thing to do is. Or, meaning to be helpful, they do not see that what they do do is not effective: "I just wanted to help," and, "Oh, well, she meant well." That may all be true, but it is not much consolation to the person who was not helped. I'm not very much impressed by my good intentions when I see that I could have been more helpful if I had paid more attention to my habits and actions. A lot of careful attention and hard work is needed to put good intentions into action in a way that will be most helpful to someone. We need to look at what we *do* as carefully and thoroughly as we look at our motives, feelings, intentions, and attitudes.

Actions Only. An action itself can be helpful, whatever the intent. Underlying feelings are not necessarily relevant: "She didn't like it one bit, but, thank goodness, she did it." "I don't care whether he is sincere or not, I just want him to behave fairly." The job gets done, a needed or desired action is performed. Similarly, there is nothing necessarily wrong with clearly stated tit-for-tat relationships: "I'll do this only if you do that," or, "You scratch my back, I'll scratch yours." The big concern of each person may be selfish, but the arrangement is workable and the actions are helpful.

Neither is it necessarily damaging to act in ways that do not match inner feelings or attitudes. There are probably many times when we all need to do that. Besides, the feelings or the inner orientation can change to match the behavior. When people feel a choice, there is a tendency toward what is called cognitive consistency, with the cognitions, or what is going on in the head, coming to match or to be consistent with the behavior: "As a person behaves, so the person becomes." Thus, for example, by forcing ourselves to behave patiently in spite of the impatience we feel, we may come to feel more patient. (If we try to force someone else, a boomerang is likely.)

Actions and Care. Can actions and care be separated? Actions without a giving attitude can be helpful. However, can the helpful actions really be as meaningful as possible without care or desire to give? And the other side of this question, Can there be genuine care without action? Does it make sense to say that you care when you do not act? If forced to choose between *receiving* action without care or care without action, which would you choose? If forced to *offer* care without action or action without care, which would you choose? Is prayer a helpful action? Personally, I do believe that care and prayer can be helpful to another person, even if that person does not know of my care and prayer. However, there are many positions on such matters. It is obvious that it is a cop-out of some sort to assume that all that is necessary is to sit back and care and pray. Thinking only, "Of course I care!" can be a false security blanket that leads us not to look for opportunities for meaningful actions. People who really care can usually find a way to show they care.

Both actions and care are useful. Just as real care is likely to lead to actions, actions are likely to be more effective when there is an inner attitude of caring intent. With intent, we are more likely to spot opportunities for useful actions. When Nan mentioned her dental surgery scheduled for the next week, the group expressed sympathy. Only Cathy called the next day to offer to drive her to and from the ordeal. Curiously, Cathy was the only one of the group scheduled to work from nine to five on the fearful day of surgery. Yet she cared enough to see the need and to try to meet it, even if that meant loss of pay. The attitude of intent to be helpful leads to spotting ways to be helpful and is likely to lead to differences in how the actions are carried out. An obvious example is that a needed action with a frown can do the job that needs doing, but the same behavior with a genuine smile can do so much more as well. Also, there often are subtle differences in our facial or bodily expressions, or in how we do the job, depending on what we are feeling. People often think they are hiding their feelings, when they are not. A tone of voice, a tilt of the head or shoulders, a shift of the eyes or of facial muscles can all communicate feelings.

Thus, effective nurture is highly likely to include an inner feeling or orientation of care and intent to be helpful, which is matched with external actions. We cannot expect from ourselves or from others the perfect combination of pure care and perfect action. But with attention to both the inner and the outer levels of nurture, we can become more effective. With the aim of developing nurturant care combined with action, we can have more relationships that are meaningful and we can deepen our understanding of nurture, while contributing to our own growth and that of others. Both loving care and effective action take a lot of hard work.

KNOWING AND CARING

Knowledge of Ourselves and Others. To nurture effectively, we need to know what we are doing. One aspect of the hard work of effective nurture is developing knowledge. We need to know ourselves and what we can give, as well as what the other person needs. Much effort is wasted when we try to give what we cannot, or what the other does not want. Even when we know or guess at the fitting action, there is no guarantee that we have the specific skills or the related traits and needs. For example, Eva wanted very much to help out in Jeanne's hospital room. Although she tried to put her uneasiness about hospitals out of her mind, she had to keep leaving the room to throw up. She added to the confusion instead of helping. However, Eva was very comfortable working with cars. She had enough sense to change the form of her nurture. When Jeanne got out of the hospital, the old clunker she had been worrying about was running very well. Making the change meant that Eva had to have the courage to admit what she could not do and to accept what she could do. It also meant stopping to think beyond the immediate situation and knowing of Jeanne's concern about the ailing car. Many other people persist in trying to give what they cannot, and miss the chance to give what they can. If there is a responsibility to nurture others, there is also a responsibility to know and to accept ourselves and those we seek to help.

Knowledge and Caring. Knowledge and caring go together—real knowing leads to care, and care leads to more knowing. All people are lovable if you know them. There are people about whom I feel like this: there is no in-between with this one, I'd have to love her in order to like her. If I choose to make the effort (and it does take effort) to get to know such a one, I do come to love and to like. I couldn't stand some of my friends if I did not care for them. This is not a matter of love being blind in friendships or in romantic relationships. It is a matter of seeing and knowing the inner strength and beauty of the person, and speaking to that strength and beauty.

The association works the other way too. When we care, we look for information about the people we care for. We want to know about them and to know them. We want them to know us. Important hurts in caring relationships sometimes involve one person not paying attention or thinking enough to know what is needed. The other feels unloved. Everyday comments reflect an awareness of this interplay of knowledge and care: "If you really cared for me, you'd know what I want." "It seems like she ought to know I wanted her there!" Comments of self-blame indicate guilt at failure to match care with knowledge: "If only I'd known you wanted that! I should have known." "I just wasn't paying attention the way I should have been."

Real caring and knowing are not just a matter of knowing what the other consciously wants. Sometimes it can mean knowing other people better than they know themselves, and sticking your neck out to act on that care and knowledge. One friend, Denny, persisted on "facilitating an adoption," as she called it. I called it, "deciding I needed a cat so one of her new kittens could have a home." For a long time, I protested Denny's hints and suggestions that I take a kitten. I had a dog who was used to being the center of attention, and, in addition, was old and deserved to remain in center stage. Besides, I did not like cats! Despite my protests, I ended up with a lovable furry feline addition to the household. I have become a cat lover as well as a dog lover. My understanding of myself and the world has increased as well as my everyday joy. When I see the aging dog and playful kitten kissing each other, and see them lying together, sleeping peacefully, I know that Denny knew more than I did. She knew more about me (and about dogs and cats) than I did, and was true to her own insights. In some ways, she also loved and knew me more than I loved and knew myself. She took more effort to prepare me for the death of my doggy than I had done for myself.

LOVING SELF AND OTHERS

Strong people love strongly. A strong mature love requires a strong mature person. The stronger and more mature you are as a person, the greater your capacity to care for others effectively. As growth continues, love increases. In turn, love given and love received foster additional growth. Thus, love and growth, self and others, all go together. The more you grow, the better you can love me. The more I grow, with the help of your love, the better I can love you and contribute to your growth, and so on, in a positive spiral. In this sense, giving to other people is as selfish as it is unselfish. On the other hand, receiving from others is unselfish, just as it is selfish.

Self-Love. We have a right, a need, and an obligation to receive love from other people, and to give love. It is equally true that we have a right, a need, and an obligation to love ourselves. Jewish and Christian scriptures say, "Love your neighbor *as yourself*." Attempting to love others without self-love and having received love is more likely to harm others than to help them. When this is true, we see other people as we need to see them to feel good about ourselves. We may see only their actual or imagined faults or their actual or imagined strengths. In either case, we do not see them as they really are, and so cannot give to them as effectively as we could otherwise. Thus, we give *from our own neediness* rather than *to their needs.* This means we need to increase our self-knowledge and our self-love, working toward a personal anchoring.

Personal Anchoring. Many people, particularly women, resist accepting the fact that they are the center of their support system. Or, as one woman said, "You are the only person who will never leave you." This means, among other things, that we must increasingly learn to count on ourselves rather than on other people for nurture and support, love and strength. It means being anchored in ourselves and not being desperate in neediness to give to or to get from other people. Knowing and accepting ourselves is hard work. It can be frightening also. Without the knowledge, we try to give what we cannot. Without the acceptance, we try to win acceptance from others rather than being free to nurture them or to take the nurture they offer. Being our own anchor means we are not dependent on other people to justify our existence or fill our lives. With internal anchoring, we are not victims of the winds of fate or the whims of others. We can tackle earnestly the task of being ourselves and fulfilling our own mission in life. Our life mission and desire for growth can include nurturing others. Freedom *from* others enables the freedom *to* give to them and to receive from them more effectively and meaningfully.

A MODEL OF NURTURE

Jesus is often cited as a model of effective love. This is quite right by psychological standards, whatever may be a person's theological views. He demonstrated effective nurture in the concrete reality of the nitty-gritty of life. His nurture was not restricted to his blood family, nor to the "right" people. At a time when other men saw women as property, he saved their lives or chatted by the village well. Nor did he expect women to confine themselves to "women's work," or know only drudgery. Mary was not censured for "talking with the men" instead of being in the kitchen with her sister. He rewarded the Syrophoenician woman's humor, even though it was somewhat at his expense. Because of his love and understanding of people and because of the effectiveness of his actions in dealing with them, the first stone was not cast at the adulteress. He responded to very specific practical needs, so that he provided wine for a party and cooked breakfast for hungry fishermen.

Although Jesus is not typically considered a model of self-love, there are clear signs of his self-anchoring. He valued his "support system," and was impatient that his friends dozed when he needed them. Yet he gave himself time apart from others to get to know himself and to rest. Until awakened by his fearful friends, he slept in the boat instead of staying awake to help in the voyage. We may not have the knowledge or powers of Jesus, but if we take seriously the aim of modeling our life after his, we will become more effective in nurture.

With improvement in the everyday practicalities and experience of giving and receiving nurture, there will be growth in a bigger or more abstract sense. A book about nurture is also a book about personal growth in a more general sense. With improved nurture, we can help ourselves and one another in the struggle to be human, and lead more fulfilled, effective lives. In the next chapter, we will look at some of the things that affect our relationships with one another.

CHAPTER 2

Why Support:
People Need People

According to a popular song, people who need people are the luckiest people in the world. According to psychological theory and evidence, we all are among the luckiest. To thrive rather than merely to survive, people continually need social relationships for giving and receiving nurture. Knowing ourselves and others involves understanding social needs. Loving ourselves and others involves accepting those needs and working to get them met.

SOCIAL NEEDS

PERSONALITY GROWTH:
NEEDS TO RECEIVE AND GIVE LOVE

From infancy on, people have social needs, and feel better about themselves and the world when those needs are met. In early life, survival physically and psychologically requires receiving love and attention. The needs to receive continue in many forms. Abraham Maslow maintained that the need to belong and to be loved is a basic human need. Food, water, and safety are needed for growth. So also, we need affection, belongingness, a friend, a sweetheart, a spouse, children, or a place in a group. Maslow suggested that there is a profound hunger for contact and togetherness that has been worsened by the scattering of families, urbanization, and the general shallowness of American friendship. In his view, we also need recognition and appreciation from other people and a feeling of importance for positive traits. If the needs are not met, we feel inferior, weak, helpless. If they are met, we feel self-confident and worthy, useful and necessary in the world.

With increasing maturity, it becomes increasingly important to give to other people and to be related through mature love. Mature love is given more for the sake of *giving* love than for the sake of *receiving* love. This giving itself is a selfish need. Without giving freely, we are blocked in our growth to maturity as well as blocked in our expression of maturity. We need to give. Mature love is a characteristic of maturity, a necessity for being truly human, and a way to find meaning in life. Yet maturity and mature love are hard to achieve. If that were not the case, this book would be much shorter. We need the input of other people if we are to grow and to give freely to them. If our needs to receive are not met, our expressions of needs to give are distorted or blocked.

INSTRUMENTAL NEEDS

The general needs to give or to receive can take the specific forms of both instrumental needs and emotional needs for contact with people. Other people may be *instrumental* in providing the help and the information that get jobs done. Sometimes another pair of hands is needed, or a ride to the car repair shop. Who is a good dentist? Does the widget go in before the gizmo? Is brand X worth the higher price? How can I deal with Dale who dumps work on me? When such needs for information are met, they are easily taken for granted.

When they are not met, there is a sense of being lost, alone, or useless.

Information from other people is needed also to satisfy a very powerful need for self-evaluation: "Is something wrong with me that I do not understand what this book is all about?" "Am I really as nurturing as I think?" Think of the relief you have felt to hear of another person's confusion: "You feel that way too! I thought I was the only one!" People also give information about unknown or unaccepted assets: "Do you really think I'm good at that? I thought I was just average." The self-assessment often involves comparison with other people, even when there are relatively tangible products involved, such as money, grades, professional advancement, or getting a toaster to work. How good is good? We need information about other people in order to have information about ourselves. By giving us information about themselves, other people are useful to us.

CONTACT NEEDS

For this category of needs, people are important for the social contact they provide. Of course, they can meet needs for contact while they are giving information or help. The term "contact comfort" came to be used after the psychologist Harry Harlow found that infant monkeys preferred an artificial "mother" who was covered with cuddly, warm, terry cloth, over the bare, cold, wire "mother" who fed them. They sat on the wire mother to eat (the food provided by the human researchers), but then went to the cloth mother. The cloth mother offered more comfort of contact. Human beings also need physical contact, or touch. For example, heart patients have a better recovery if they have a dog, presumably because a dog is easy to touch. Touch may be more important in meaningful sexual activity than is sexual release. Some people manage to have sex relations without really

touching, without making psychological contact, and
without enjoying the sensation of touch. The absence of
human touch has been suggested as the source of loneliness. Try an experiment. The next time you are lonely
and blue, hug yourself. It is not as helpful as having
someone else hug you comfortably, but it is better than
nothing.

The concept of contact comfort has come to be used
more generally to refer to just being with people as
people. The idea is that people need to associate with
people, even without physical touch or without an exchange of information. Associating with other people
does have good effects, particularly in times of stress. For
example, women with difficult pregnancies had fewer
complications when they gave birth if they felt they had
support. Male executives who had the stress of having to
move because of their jobs had fewer physical disorders
if they had good support. Compared with those who
developed physical disorders, they had a strong commitment to themselves, their uniqueness, and their work,
and they had support from others in this. Also, just being
with strangers helps reduce anxiety during catastrophes
(such as the 1965 electrical blackout in New York City
and the earthquake in Los Angeles in 1971).

Differences in People. Some people have trouble clearly admitting and acting on their needs, while others are
quite comfortable doing so. Generally, the need to be
with people is more obvious in people who are firstborn
or only children than in others, and in women than in
men. However, later-borns and men are not lacking in
this need so much as being simply less comfortable
acting directly on it. For example, the firstborn men
interviewed after an earthquake reported *less* anxiety but
helped *more* people than did the later-born men. Although they were avoiding admitting their desire to
associate, they nonetheless got their emotional needs for

contact met in instrumental ways. Offering help is more approved for men than admitting the human experience: "I'm scared."

Unmet Needs. Women too pay the price for living in a society in which the need of adults for contact with other adults is not clearly recognized and admitted. Women as well as men often hold back from expressing their need for contact. Often a person may not even be aware of having the need. There is a false view that it is childish to want just to be around other people. Adults may wait patiently, with needs unmet, for a "cover story" or "adult excuse," so that they state an instrumental need of some business or thing to be done. Without a cover story, they hold back from making contact with others. When they do have one, the story may not make sense to others, or may mislead them, keep them from seeing the underlying need for contact. Thus, if you wait to call with a specific question, you may find the question answered quickly and you never get the contact you need because you misled the person you called. You stated what the psychologists call a socioemotional need as an instrumental one.

FACTORS AFFECTING ACQUAINTANCESHIP

Although people need people, we get to know only some people, and want to be friends with some but not with others. Generally, we want to get needs met and have positive feelings from associating with other people, including the good feelings of giving to them. How do the feelings develop? Understanding some of the factors that generally influence getting acquainted and liking can help us see why we like some people but not others, and can alert us to how we may miss getting to know people whom we could have important nurturing relationships with. Also, by knowing what is important to people, we can be in a better position to be supportive to them.

SOME BASIC FACTORS

Proximity and Mere Exposure. You cannot become friends and give to or receive from somebody with whom you have no contact. The greater the proximity or physical nearness, the greater the likelihood of becoming acquainted, particularly when the people regard each other as equals. For example, in an apartment complex, ratings of knowing and liking another person were related to how closely people lived to one another. One exception was that people who lived near the mailboxes knew and were known by an increased number of people! Similarly, blacks and whites assigned to the same apartment building became better friends than did the people assigned to different buildings in the same complex. Thus, accidents of life that bring strangers together can lead to certain people becoming friends.

Being physically close allows exposure, which is important itself. Simply being around the other person can lead to liking the person. The *mere exposure effect* is that, generally, the more you see or hear unfamiliar sights or sounds, the more you like them, particularly if you did not originally have intense dislike. With music, for example, "Now, that I've heard it, I kind of like it." We get used to whatever is around. This includes people. With people, the exposure can also mean a chance to discover that "she's just a person too," or "oh, she's not so bad when you get used to her." This may involve seeing the person's distinctive, unique beauty and strength. What is more clear is the importance of discovering some of the things we have in common with the other and having good feelings about ourselves.

Similarity. With greater proximity and exposure, people are more likely to discover ways in which they are alike. Similarity is an extremely important and powerful factor affecting people's preference in their choice of associates. Friendships between children and between adults are related to similarities in family income, interests, hobbies, general intelligence and educational level and goals, political preferences—and almost any similarity imaginable.

People who are similar are attracted to each other. During association, people also tend to become more alike, and to overestimate how alike they are. That is, the more like somebody we are, the more we're likely to like her; and the more we like her, the more likely we are to think that we are more alike than we really are. We like to think that people who are important to us agree with us, and generally are similar to us, as well as like us. It may be true that "everyone I know agrees with me," but you are likely to overestimate the amount of agreement and you are not as likely to know people who disagree as you are to know people who agree. On the other hand, you may dislike someone because you do not think the person agrees with you!

Values and Dangers of Similarity. We like to think we are right. Similar people who agree with us help us think that. That is reinforcing. This is not just a matter of conceit, though that is not irrelevant! We need to think we have information about ourselves and about the world. To meet the need for self-evaluation, we need other people and often they must be similar to us in some ways. Comparison with dissimilar others gives faulty information that can make us feel bad unnecessarily. A person who has a maid is of no use to me in understanding my attempts to juggle many other demands against those of housekeeping. Nor is a person with a full-time secretary relevant to my needs to understand how I stack up in handling all my work activities. To know whether I am really as bad as I think, I need to compare myself with similar others, not with dissimilar people who have major differences in their lives. Although I know that, I do sometimes go ahead and feel bad anyway. It is easier to *talk* about being realistic than to *be* it! Knowing someone who does not have a maid or a secretary helps me to keep perspective and reminds me that I'm okay.

More generally, we need the security of feeling that we know what reality is all about. With the agreement of others, we can think we know what is going on. If someone disagrees, is it "just differences of opinion"? Or is that person misinformed, crazy, or stupid? Or am I? Disagreement or dissimilarity can cause confusion. People prefer to avoid confusion.

There is a danger in avoiding confusion. As long as we are surrounded by people who agree with us (so we think), we do not have to stop and think about the issue anymore. For example, associating with similar others can provide a comforting relief that there is no need to take "those other people" seriously. Our biases and limitations in thinking are not challenged. Growth is blocked. Some people are so uptight that when a discussion of different points of view gets started, they quickly end it with, "Oh, well, people differ, each to his or her own opinion." What is being shown is not an open-minded tolerance of others' views, but fear of having one's own views challenged. The lack of agreement is pushed out of the way. This prevents learning from the differences of view and keeps people from expressing themselves and feeling that their own views count.

Self-Esteem. What if you have a very low opinion of yourself—little self-esteem? Do you best like someone who shares your low view of yourself or someone who disagrees and thinks well of you? Receiving positive input is more important. However, it's hard for people with low esteem to ask for support and it is also hard for someone to offer them support. They turn people off because often they seem aloof, or to have a holier-than-thou attitude. That is a protection against being hurt more, as they have been in the past. A sense of small self-worth usually develops from bad experiences with people. Then they have trouble believing the positive feedback they so desperately want. They may need to be hit over the head with the fact that they are liked and valued. They may hound you for continual assurance. Patience pays. With genuine reassurance from others they trust, they do grow to like themselves. And they become very effective in nurturing others.

Physical Attractiveness. People do not like to think they judge others or themselves on the basis of something so "superficial" as physical appearance. But they do, without realizing it. Physical appearance comes into all sorts of judgments, from selecting a date or mate to jury decisions, and estimates of a child's intelligence. Generally, "beauty is best." However, in long friendships and marriages, people tend to be generally about the same in physical attractiveness. Although attractiveness brings many rewards, people are sometimes afraid to approach those who are more attractive than they because they expect rejection from them or do not think such attractive people need any help. One result is that very attractive people can be lonelier and more in need of support than those who are "just average." Also, an extremely beautiful woman sometimes is considered superficial or immoral because of her beauty. Thus, most people can benefit from a compliment about their physical appearance and will tend to like someone who compliments them sincerely. However, extremely attractive people, particularly women, may instead need a reminder that they are valued for themselves.

PERSONALITY TRAITS

Basically, we like people who help us feel good about
the world and about ourselves. Exactly what kind of
person that is depends upon our own needs, traits, and
interests. And we may like different people for different
reasons. They may meet different needs or help us feel
better in different ways. For example, people prefer an
extrovert as "a fun person to be with." Introverts increase
in value when the search is for "a friend to trust." We
may value one friend because she is optimistic and
makes us laugh, but we may be very annoyed with her
when we think she is not taking a serious issue seriously.
We generally like people who say positive things about
us, unless we find out they are insincere. The two
personality traits discussed next are related to the
amount of comfort we can feel with another person.

Self-Disclosure. Have you had times when there was
really good sharing? You may have noticed that you
talked more than you usually do. This may be a matter of
"just clicking right together" at a particular time. It may
also mean that the other person is generally high on self-
disclosure. Self-disclosure means making one's self
known. People who show themselves as they are come to
be liked more than others. One person being "honest and
open," and showing herself as "a real person," is likely to
encourage the other person to be that way as well.
Sensitive self-disclosure enables one to discover similarities at deep, intimate levels and develop trust. Low
disclosers seem distrustful of themselves and others, as if
afraid of being known. High disclosers are willing to be
open and forthright about themselves. Perhaps they are
liked because they show their humanness, with all the
frailties of that. That makes it easy for us to relate to them
"as people" and to feel not so bad about what we know to
be our own foibles and weaknesses. With the courage to
be ourselves and to show ourselves, we discover the

personness of one another and experience positive input at deeper levels than usual.

There are, of course, some cultural rules. Discussing intimate feelings is not always appropriate, and people who carelessly reveal more than the other person wants to know are bores or embarrassments. However, there are probably more people who are too hesitant to share themselves than there are who burden others inappropriately with self-disclosures. Some sensitivity is needed about exactly how much when. The self-anchored person has this sensitivity as well as the courage to disclose.

Dogmatism. Some people "disclose" in a limited and superficial way—they are very ready to announce their views about the way the world is and what is right. However, they are not willing to listen to other people's views. They are dogmatic. Dogmatism is closed-mindedness. Dogmatic people are more likely than others to avoid discussing issues when there are differences of opinion. Although dogmatic people are liked at first, they are disliked after a while. Perhaps at first it seems they are self-confident and know where they stand. It takes a while for you to realize that they do not care where *you* stand! And, wherever that is, if it is not the same as where they are, you are wrong. Any nurture they offer is limited and perhaps false. They cannot really see you as you are and thus cannot accept that your needs may be different from what they pronounce your needs to be.

WOMEN SUPPORTING WOMEN

Many pressures work against women supporting one another. Women are not valued as much as men, and friendships are not valued as much as the tangible outcomes of achievement in the workplace. Thus, women and friends take second place to men and work. Friendships between women have a double whammy against them. And women often make the problem worse than it needs to be by undercutting themselves and other women. Some of the ways the pressures are shown are in terms of the basic factors of interpersonal relationships just discussed.

SOME BASIC FACTORS

Proximity and Exposure. Social practices generally reduce the likelihood that women can have the contact with each other that could enable supportive relationships in either the work world or the social world. Things are changing, but they are not yet changed. Whatever their life-style, women tend to have their hands full taking care of the job at hand. Many women go about the business of tending to the details of arranging the children's car pool or the husband's office party without stopping to notice the chance of developing relationships with the other women who are involved. In many work settings, there are still few women. A woman bakery owner, accounting professor, or manager of a computer store is likely to be surrounded by more men than women. When there are other women around the shop, job pressures can make it hard to develop the supportive relationships with women that could reduce the work pressures.

Women's Attitude Toward Women. Are women worth the effort? Even when contact is made, there often is a put-down attitude toward the other woman. After all, she is "just a woman." Consider your reactions to discovering that a woman, not a man, has been assigned to fix your car, to work on your taxes, to fly you across the country, or to operate on your child. Are you really as confident that the job will be done right as you were when you expected a man to do it? It is easy to *say* yes. If a male nurse or a male professional housecleaner appears, is he expected to do a better job than a woman would, even at a "woman's job"? It is easy to say *no*.

Research shows that both women and men tend to see men as more competent than women in doing a task, whether the task is a "feminine" or a "masculine" one. Women are said to owe success to luck or to an easy task, or occasionally to trying harder. Neither women nor men have learned to think of a woman as being "as good as a man." The learning experiences of a lifetime are not erased easily. Many women have such negative views of women without realizing it. Things are changing, but it is unrealistic to expect that many years of experience can be offset immediately. Women with such an attitude have little encouragement to look to other women for support.

Similarity, Trust, and Physical Attractiveness. With all the pressures, there is little opportunity to discover similarities. With the negative evaluations of women and of oneself, there is diminished reason to value similar others: "What can a woman offer me?" In addition, traditional practices have encouraged women to define themselves through the attention of and the approval of men. Thus, women have been put in the position of being competitors for that approval. The competition does not foster supportive relationships. Why associate with the enemy? Why be honest and open with another woman if her best interest calls for her using that against you? Why confide your feelings of inadequacies to some- one who might be trying to steal "your man"?

Women also often undo each other on the matter of physical attractiveness. When an interesting-looking woman walks into a meeting, do other women think, "What an attractive woman—I'd really like to get to know her"? Often, the comments are something like: "Who on earth is she?" "She's really after the boss." "She must have been primping all afternoon." Is an older woman "no spring chicken," while an equally old man is "distinguished"? Does a woman have wrinkles and a man have character lines? When women are seen only in relation to men, so that they are rivals for men's attention and approval, it is difficult to develop and bring to fruition the basic conditions that encourage a respectful association with other women or with oneself.

SELF-ANCHORING, OR DEFINITION THROUGH OTHERS?

In many respects, women are the worst enemies of themselves as individuals, and of each other as a group. Women have gotten the same broad cultural messages about women that other people have. Because women and relationships are not taken seriously in society as a whole, women tend to devalue themselves and other women. This has been called an *identification with the aggressor*. It happens especially when a person feels dependent upon a very powerful other who can withhold reward and offer punishment. The logic is something like, "If you can't beat them, join them." This includes adopting their standards as one's own. The alternative is to reduce dependency on the other by affirming oneself as a person, and developing self-anchoring and a personal definition of who one is. This is hard to do by oneself. Self-affirmation is easier if one has the support of similar other people who are valued. Women are in a particularly advantageous position to support other women. To value other women is itself a breakthrough requiring courage and a personal self-definition. More and more women are choosing to affirm themselves and to support other women, and to grow individually and together. Women are recognizing and claiming their rights to their own needs as women and to their own rights to the growth they are expected to foster in men and children. To do this well, women must love themselves. The next chapter deals with the value and necessity of self-love.

CHAPTER 3

I'm a Person Too!
Self-Love and Growth

Lack of self-love is one of the biggest problems that interferes with good intentions to be a nurturing person. With self-love, nurture is a gift. Without it, it is a price to pay to feel loved by others. Because so many people do not love themselves really well, this theme deserves continuing attention.

THE NECESSITY OF SELF-LOVE

"Love your neighbor as yourself." Curiously, "as yourself" is often forgotten. Half-truths can be very misleading! Attempts to love others are futile without self-love. We are also told, "Judge not, that you be not judged." Yet how often we judge ourselves negatively for self-love and positively for lack of it. In part because of little self-love, our judgments of ourselves are often far more extreme than are our judgments of others. Self-love is biblical and logical as well as very practical and necessary for loving others. Let's look quickly at the general logic and then at some of the more everyday practicalities.

SELF-LOVE MAKES SENSE

Logic. If I am to love others but not myself, then others, too, are to love others (including me) but not themselves (and they are the ones I am told to love). This does not make much sense. Why should I not be love-worthy from my own perspective when I am love-worthy from the perspective of those I love? Isn't that a put-down of loved ones? It amounts to saying: "I love you, but you have lousy tastes! I do not respect your judgment in loving me." Does God love me less than God loves other people? Not thinking more highly of myself than I ought is not a proscription against self-love. In fact, if I feel that I am the only one God does not love, I am being rather arrogant in singling myself out as the exception to the rule. If God loves me, why should I pronounce myself unlovable? If others, whom God loves, also love me, who do I think I am that I should not love myself? The logic is hidden in the cultural confusion about the meaning of love, self, and selfishness.

Selfishness. Real love encourages what is most produc-tive for human growth. This is true whether the love is directed to ourselves or to others. The more growthful our attitudes toward ourselves, the more we can love others. Thus Erich Fromm argues that self-love and love of others go together, and the combined love is the opposite of selfishness.

No: self-love versus other love

Yes: (self-love + other love) versus selfishness

Selfish people are incapable of loving others, but they are also incapable of loving themselves. The apparent overabundance of care for self is an attempt to hide and to make up for lack of genuine care for self. They are unhappy, anxious people of hidden self-hate and self-contempt, desperately trying to snatch superficial satis-factions while being blocked from deeper satisfactions. Some people have to put down other people rather than praising and speaking to their strengths. This is because they do not love themselves healthily. They feel that strengthening others is weakening themselves. They are not free to love others, because they are not free to love themselves. In the same way, though it appears different at first glance, making a big display of unselfishness often is a mask for selfishness, such as with people who expect love and admiration from other people for the sake of their supposed unselfishness. Without self-love, they have to go to unusual lengths to feel any love. Without self-love, they do not know themselves or others.

Love and Knowledge. Productive loving requires knowing the person. In Fromm's view, it is objective knowing in the sense that we see the person as the person really is rather than according to our own needs. It is subjective knowing in the sense that we have a personal relatedness to the loved one rather than only seeing from a distance, as if the person were a thing. The creative energy devoted to the loved one enlivens and changes that person for the better.

This holds for loving and knowing oneself as well as others. We can, and often do, see ourselves as we need to see ourselves rather than as we really are. We can also see ourselves from an uncaring distance, as a thing, judging the thing severely against an unrealistic standard of perfection, without the love and compassion, understanding and reasonableness offered to other people. Ironically this judgmental self-blame often convinces us that we are good people because we are so stern with ourselves about being bad. This self-judgment and lack of self-love is the same as trying to out-God God, condemning ourselves and then patting ourselves on the back because we have done so. Neither the condemnation nor the pat helps us to love others.

WAYS OF RELATING TO PEOPLE

Like Fromm, Karen Horney (pronounced HORN-eye) saw healthy self-love as necessary for nurturing relationships. Her views help show how relationships with other people can be disturbed and troubled, rather than harmonious and natural, because of fear and lack of self-love. Conflicts with others develop when we have conflicts within ourselves.

NEEDS AND SELF-LOVE

Balance of Three Orientations. Horney said that people have three major ways in which they need to relate to people. We need to express each of these three different orientations of our personalities. With healthy self-love, each basic human need is accepted and more or less equally expressed. Without self-acceptance, one or two ways are developed to extreme. Problems arise when there is not a balanced expression of the three styles or strategies for relating to people.

Moving toward people is an affiliative orientation, or, in extreme, one of dependency, compliance, and self-effacement, with excessive concern about pleasing others. *Moving away from people* involves taking time for one's self and being self-sufficient. In the extreme, it is detachment from others and resignation, seeing one's self as above the mundane of others' petty concerns. *Moving against people* is essentially self-assertion, standing up for oneself, not being pushed around. In extreme form, it is aggression—combative, competitive, dominating, delighting in defeating or putting other people down.

All of these orientations are natural, normal, human tendencies. With personal security, and self-acceptance, each is accepted and expressed. Then they balance each other, so that no one becomes extreme. In relatively healthy form, they keep each other in perspective, so to speak. Because a tendency to move in another direction pulls it back, any move in one direction does not go too far. For example, acting to please other people is balanced by the urges to take time for ourselves and to not let others push us around. Trouble happens when any orientation becomes too extreme.

Nurture and Dependence. Horney was concerned that women tend to define themselves too much in the orientation of moving toward people: "I am just here to serve and to please." It might seem that a person with an extreme "toward" orientation would be very good in nurturing. In fact, "Balance is best" is the rule. For two reasons, an extreme "toward" orientation reduces the effectiveness of nurture. First, when not balanced by the other needs, the need to move toward others can be actually self-defeating and self-destructive. There is a strong dependence on them, with much worry and fretting about the others' disapproving or leaving. That itself keeps us from seeing clearly and nurturing well. In the extreme, mistreatment or even physical abuse can be accepted in order to keep the "togetherness." Loving oneself and accepting oneself reduce the likelihood of being at the mercy of others and doing anything they ask just to please them.

Second, the other side of the coin is that with an extreme development of only this affiliation orientation, other people are put in awkward positions. If I can relate to you only by moving toward you, you must be there for me, without concern for your own needs. I must give to you or be protected by you, even if that is not what you want. Signs that you may care for someone or something else, as well as for me, are extremely threatening.

Sometimes people do mesh, in that one person's extreme dependency and self-effacement may match with

the other person's extreme need to protect or to dominate. If neither person decides to grow, the relationship
can last for quite a while. In fact, probably many marriages last because the imbalance of one person meshes
with the imbalance of the other. In many relationships,
however, the other person is likely to resist some of the
extreme, unrealistic expectations. This is felt as rejection
and increases the fear, which increases the demands for
assurance, which increases the fear, and so on. The more
unrealistic demands are rebuffed, the more fear of rejection is increased, so the demands for assurance are more
intensified—a *vicious circle* in which the attempt to
correct the problem creates a greater problem, and so the
faulty solution is pressed into service yet again.

Nurture and Self-Sufficiency. Strong overconcern with
serving others can also be part of holding an unrealistic
view of self-sufficiency. A woman with an overdeveloped
self-sufficiency view sees herself as not needing for
herself the kind of nurture she offers to others. She gives
help while being above needing help: "I do not need
you, but you need me." She does, of course, need help
from others, but does not say so. By giving to others from
her tower of strength, she is able to relate to others and
have some of her own dependency needs met. The
problem is that she is not clear with herself or with
others. She has to receive while pretending not to. The
enjoyment of giving to others and being with them is
diminished because she is not clearly admitting her need
of others.

Self-Rejection and the Glorious Image. Why does an
exaggeration of one orientation develop? When it does,
why can it not be corrected easily and quickly? The
habits of a lifetime cannot be changed overnight. Self-
rejection cannot be switched easily to self-acceptance.
When people feel insecure, they find a way of acting so
that they feel loved by others and secure with them. That

one way becomes their main way of relating to people. One way or strategy works reasonably well, and so the other ways are ignored. Imbalance results. This usually starts during childhood, though the same process can be started in adulthood as well.

We easily come to feel we *have* to behave that one way if others are to accept us. This means that we have to ignore other parts of ourselves, and then gradually come to dislike or to disown those parts. Behavior can get very unnatural, unrealistic, and unreasonable. In the process of convincing ourselves that we are really okay, we build a Glorious Image of ourselves and try to convince ourselves and others that we are that. Positive interpretations are given for negative habits. Faults are twisted into virtues. Instead of saying, "I'm a submissive person," it is, "I'm sensitive to others' feelings and want to please them." Similarly, domination may get called a competitive spirit, and detachment is thought of as being above petty everyday matters, perhaps "otherworldly." These are distortions of the truth, or illusions to protect the Glorious Image that develops. The more we try to be that Glorious Image, the more we dislike and lose touch with who we really are. We may exaggerate certain actions to the point that they become a sort of addiction.

PSYCHOLOGICAL ADDICTIONS

The Obvious and the Not So Obvious. Drugs, including caffeine, nicotine, alcohol, and over-the-counter and prescription drugs, are obvious means of addiction. Using them seems to be a selfish pampering of one's self, but is a statement that love of self is absent or weak. When the momentary comfort given by the drug is gone, then guilt, fear, confusion, or boredom comes, to be relieved by more of the drug. This is one variety of a vicious circle. Any kind of action can be addictive. Watching television to relax can become a desperate need. Soap operas exposing other people's lives may become more important than one's own life.

Clearly, positive behavior can be addictive too. Look at the workaholic. The work may be brought home from the office, or discovered or invented in the home. Keeping busy for the sake of keeping busy is a general workaholic attitude. Even leisure becomes work as we work at keeping busy having fun. Idle hands may be the devil's workshop, but you can't hold hands with God or with people if your hands are always moving, moving, moving.

People—having to be with them, or having to do good things for them—can be used for addictive purposes. Cultural images encourage women to addiction to domestic activities and doing things for others, even if the other people do not want things done for them: "I must knit a scarf for Chris." The shiny kitchen floor can become more important than the human beings served by the kitchen, and the perfect soufflé can become more important than human desires for some old-fashioned mashed potatoes. Other people may praise the skill of handmade gifts, the devotion to work, and the cleanliness next to godliness. They encourage the addiction without realizing what they are doing. The behavior becomes more and more unreasonable and desperately needed as a way of getting love and admiration from others: "This worked once, so try, try again!" Such behavior is not necessarily physically self-destructive. However, it can be destructive psychologically. The behavior, otherwise neutral or useful, comes to be a compulsive drive that must be expressed.

Compulsion and Choice. The crucial element is not the specific behavior, such as taking tranquilizers or waxing the floor. Rather, the important issue is whether there is choice. With addictive behavior, the ability to make a choice gradually erodes. There is a feeling of "must" or "have to," with a desperation to carry out the addictive behavior. Discrimination and realism are lost. One television show is as good as another, Chris will freeze without a fifth knitted scarf, germs will take over the house if the shine on the floor is not polished. We also see the lack of discrimination about people. Someone will get a knitted scarf, it does not really matter who. Also, people with strong addictions to people may have to have a special friend or lover, but it does not really matter who the person is. Thus they are likely to make unwise choices about whom they select, because they are not really selecting, they are just taking the first person who happens to come along.

What would happen if such people could not engage in the addictive behavior? Their feeling often is that the world would collapse. What is expressed may be a glib, "Oh, that would be okay. I do have choice, so there's no need to choose not to." The trick on oneself is saying: "I can take it or leave it. So there. Now get out of the way and let me at it!" Thinking that the choice is there and so does not need to be demonstrated is an illusion of the Glorious Image. So also are the specific explanations and self-praise: "Chris likes my scarves," "What's wrong with a shiny floor!" or, "Television helps me relax," and "I'm the kind of person who just really likes people." By such means we avoid seeing the rejected and despised self we do not love.

"You are the only person who will never leave you." Thus, it is important to know and nurture that person who is you.

DECISIONS FOR SELF-LOVE

KNOWING WHAT YOU NEED

Knowing what you need is crucial in the growth of self-love and self-discovery. You must take yourself seriously as a loved one worth knowing and caring about. People often do not get their needs met because they do not know who they are or do not ask for what they want. Unfortunately the cultural message that women exist only to serve and nurture others takes its toll in many ways. For example, a woman who knows well how to balance the books at work and what would be the perfect addition to the home workshop can be amazingly befuddled and befuddling when asked what she wants for herself. When she does know, she may be hesitant to say so, thinking she deserves nothing: "I don't want to cause any trouble." Sometimes, women assume somthing like: "I won't get what I want anyway, so why bother asking." The next step, if the sequence continues, is, "Why bother thinking of myself and knowing what I want!" Women do have a responsibility to themselves and to others to know what they want and to ask for it. What they need can be a tangible product or a change in the behavior of themselves or of others. Improved self-love can take many forms. The solution for one may be the problem for another. What one person needs as a corrective may be what needs to be corrected for another person.

Importance of Small Changes. Simply recognizing the ways in which major orientations are being expressed can sometimes help in spotting better ways. The needed change may be a relatively small one, or a loosening up of current patterns. Looking outside the home for expressions of the "toward" orientation may be a useful step for many women, as well as a necessary step for those without a live-in family. For some women, the self-sufficiency orientation is exaggerated and so the help of well-intentioned others is refused, perhaps because "it's easier to do it myself." Sharing tasks can provide another means for togetherness, and perhaps make free time for other forms of being with people or for time alone.

Asking for What You Need. For whatever the reason,

many people do not know how to ask for what they need, or are afraid to ask. Part of the fear is that the request will cause a problem for others, or will be seen as criticism of what they have been offering. Often, other people are much more willing to listen to the request than is feared. "Help, I hurt" is reason enough for making a request. "Ouch, you're stepping on my toes" is a very legitimate message to give others. When not expressed, the hurt can hide behind a mask of anger, petty annoyance, or mysterious moodiness. The problem is not corrected, and other people are hurt as well.

Sometimes people refuse offers they want to accept. One friend said "No" three times when I offered to come early to help her with party preparations. Later, she told me how hurt she was that I did not help in her time of need. When I reminded her of my offers, she confessed that she has trouble admitting that she is not as self-sufficient as she claims. In her view, I should have known that and come. She needed to relax, ask, and accept.

Letting Go Into Care. Accepting nurture and care can be hard if you're not used to it. Women have been overtrained to say and to think that they are to nurture and not to be nurtured. Then, it is not easy to relax and enjoy being nurtured: "Oh, no, don't bother." "It doesn't matter." "It's not important." "I don't really need it." When nurture is offered to you, relax into care. Let the bed hold you, as one of my friends says. She pointed out correctly that some people cannot get a good night's sleep or rest during illness because they will not let go enough to let the bed do its job. People can be the same way when nurture and support are offered by another person. They do not "let go" to accept what others offer.

New Skills and Self-Assertion

Being Prepared. When people decide to expand themselves or to change, they are likely to encounter some practical difficulties. Although the old ways have problems that need to be corrected, they have the advantage of safety and familiarity. Change can be confusing and frightening. Other people have also become used to the "old way" and "the way you've always been." You may confuse them as much as you confuse yourself! For example, you might choose to forgo some of your former self-sufficiency and let someone help you with jobs or chores you previously thought only you could do. Or you might increase your assertiveness to get the help you wanted before: "This time, I really mean it!" They need clarity about your intent and some time to readjust their own habits. For any changes, some clarity and firmness, with oneself and others, are necessary to resist clinging to or relapsing to the old way of doing things.

Patience. Be patient with yourself and with others as you develop new personal and interpersonal skills and explore yourself. New responses are not so smooth as old ones. That means, for example, that with new learning we often overdo by making the response too intense or using it too often. When children first learn to whistle, to count past ten, or to tie bows, they whistle, count, and tie endlessly, whether or not they have what adults consider a good reason. Then the excitement of discovery dies down, and the children practice only when it is appropriate, to everyone's satisfaction. Much the same is true of adults who are developing new responses or changing from the usual. Thus, in the process of deciding not to be pushed around anymore, one may go through a phase of pushing others around, or being overly suspicious that someone is trying to do that. "You're too sensitive" is said often to those who feel that they are just now becoming sensitive enough to be aware of problems that need to be corrected.

Time Alone. How can you know what you need? How can you know when you are too sensitive or impatient or unreasonable? You would not expect to know and care for someone else without spending time with just that person. The same is true for being comfortable with yourself. There is no substitute for time alone, particularly if you have been out of touch with yourself for some time. The less you have had time alone, the more you need it. The time might be spent in a long bubble bath, a quiet evening alone, or a short drive in the country. The important thing is that it is a time for you to enjoy and to talk with yourself. Do not make the common error of feeling guilty the whole time for other things you are not doing.

This is necessary time. It allows for recovering from within some of the energy that has been given to other people in nurture and perhaps not returned. Curiously, when people are ill physically, they are allowed to miss work and to receive sympathy as well. However, taking time off to *avoid* illness is not considered responsible adult behavior! The problem is not always one of physical overwork or work stress. Often it is a matter of losing touch with oneself and not having access to the vital energy and inspiration that come from inside.

With time alone for reflection, meditation, and self-exploration, we have a better chance of coming to know and to be comfortable with ourselves. Then we can see the illusions better—the illusions that support our Glorious Image—and find the strength to know and to love ourselves. With greater love, there can be greater knowledge. The next chapter discusses self-knowledge about motives for nurture.

CHAPTER 4

Why Support:
What Are the Motives?

Offers of nurture sometimes are more confusing than really helpful. The problem may lie in the reasons for the offer. People can offer help for the wrong reasons without realizing it. This lack of knowledge may reflect lack of self-love or too much concern to be nurturing and a "good person." Defenses and illusions to protect the Glorious Image keep us from knowing our motives. Thus, our growth and our ability to nurture effectively are blocked.

CONFUSIONS IN NURTURING

SOME PROBLEM PATTERNS

People sometimes undermine their efforts and cause confusion for themselves and for the people they want to help. They seem to want to be helpful, but they also seem to have something in mind other than giving nurturing care. They give mixed messages. When you are on the receiving end, it is easy to get disoriented and conclude: "Something must be wrong with me. . . . This person is being helpful and I'm not really appreciating it!" Nurturing oneself involves seeing other people as they are. On the other hand, if people seem confused or unappreciative of the gifts you offer, perhaps you are giving mixed messages because you do not really know your motives.

Some confusing styles of nurture are listed here. If you do not see something of yourself as a giver in the descriptions, you are a perfect human being or you are not yet seeing yourself clearly. I started this list thinking of problems I see in my friends. Before long, I was thinking of my own faults as well. In each of the patterns, getting something is more important than giving, and the giver is likely to see only Virtues that protect the illusions of the Glorious Image.

The Busybody Bumblebee. Somebody with this orientation fills her life flitting around from flower to flower, offering her helpfulness. Her chief motive, really, is to keep busy being helpful. And she can be very helpful. She explores the world so much that she acquires useful information and skills. Sometimes she zings in with the perfect gift or supportive behavior that nobody else thought of. However, her efforts can also miss the mark widely, because she is more intent on being busy being helpful than attending to the person she's helping.

The Suffering Servant. When this attitude is dominant, the important motive is that the self-appointed martyr receive satisfaction for suffering. She assumes that the more she suffers, the greater should be your profit and gratitude. If you value what she gives, she is "glad to suffer for you." If you do not suitably value her offerings, you feel guilty.

"See Me." A person who has this style of operating may be so busy rushing around being important that she never does anything useful. The main concern is not nurturing, but being seen and admired. A related version is the *Token Giver.* This is a person who contributes minimally but plays that for much more than it's worth. She brags about the bag of potato chips she brought

when other people made their own casseroles or cakes.

The Efficient Robot. For this person, the central aim or feature of Glorious Image is to be calm, efficient, logical, and rational. She often arrives at a correct deduction about what is needed, and does it efficiently. However, because her attention is to the logic of the situation, she may show no zest. Also, she may miss knowing what would be most helpful, because she does not pick up intuitive information that does not fit a rational framework. Unfortunately, if she does not have a logical, rational grasp of the situation, "nothing computes," and so she does nothing. It would violate her sense of logical order to say, "I don't have the faintest idea what is going on, but what can I do?"

"Of Course I Am!" The "of course" attitude is a tip-off that the image of being supportive is a more important goal than actually being supportive. She talks a good game. If she thinks her supportive image is firm, she does not take action: "It's too bad this came up at the wrong time." But, for her, *most* times are wrong. Then she suddenly saves the day and her image with amazing thoughtfulness.

The Aloof Cynic: "Why bother? Nobody helps me." There may be people who just do not care. However, a cynical attitude usually hides hurt and pain. The cynic may be an *Unworthy Nobody* who feels rejected. An Unworthy Nobody feels that her right to live at all depends on receiving or on giving nurture. If her own needs to be nurtured have not been met, she may attempt to prove her right to exist by working incessantly in giving. If her offers are rejected, she becomes more hurt and cynical.

The Fulfilled Tape Recorder. The final type to be mentioned is one who knows all the right things to say and to do in order to avoid being seen as one of the previous types. She may have read books, including this one, or taken courses from which she got ideas about the fulfilled person. Her behavior and talk often are quite helpful and reassuring. But there is something missing— her self!

MOTIVES AND DEFENSES

The nurturant motives of the people just described are not so simple as they appear on the surface. Yet if you told them that, they would disagree strongly. You would wish you had never brought up the issue. The intense response is likely to indicate defensiveness in protecting the Virtues of the Glorious Image. Being aware of defenses can help bring understanding and patience with the help others do or do not offer. The awareness can aid in promoting understanding and patience with oneself as well.

Defenses. Defenses protect our "hot spots," or areas of weakness, vulnerability, threat, fear, anxiety. Everyone has such areas of discomfort. Everyone uses defenses, though some of us are more defensive than others. Defenses keep us from seeing ourselves as we really are. To protect us, they distort reality in some way that has to do with our felt weaknesses. With defenses working, we may "see" what we most fear, or we may "see" only what is not fearful. In either case, there is a distortion about what other people (as well as we ourselves) are doing and thinking. We interpret remarks in ways that are not realistic. We misread our own motives, and misread those of other people as well. Thus, we accuse them of neglecting us, using us, taking us for granted, and so forth. They may accuse us of the same thing! Both may be right.

Recognizing Defenses. It is not always easy to know when someone is being defensive. People develop defenses over a lifetime and so get pretty good at using them skillfully, without appearing stupid or foolish. It is particularly hard to recognize our own defenses. The reason the defenses started was to protect from pain and anxiety. If we were aware of them, they would not be doing their job of protecting us. However, there are some clues that should alert us. The stronger the defense, the more emotional and irrational or inappropriate the behavior: "She just could not understand that I did not mean to slight her!" Perhaps the speaker has stumbled over a defense in the other person, or in herself at having wanted to slight the other person without realizing it! A person whose defenses have been touched might snap angrily, "What do you mean by *that*?" In the same situation, a person not particularly defensive about the issue might ask calmly, though with confusion: "What do you mean by that? I don't understand."

Thus, generally, defensive emotionality and irrationality are shown in behavior that is compulsive, indiscriminate, or inappropriate for the circumstances. The addictions discussed in the previous chapter are specific kinds of defenses. Anyone can become alert to the clues. A caution, however, is relevant. One trick we can play on ourselves is saying, "Yes, I know I have defenses, everyone does," so that then we feel no need to look for what they are and how they influence relationships with others. Or, similarly, by admitting some faults, we make believe that we are seeing all of them. By spotting the speck of dust in one eye, we can trick ourselves into thinking that there is no log in the other eye! Although we might play tricks with ourselves, and we may not be able to see all of our own defenses, we can come to make educated guesses about when we are likely to be defending and how. And the more we love ourselves, the less defensive we need to be and the more we can see and accept our real motives.

More than One Motive. Human behavior often is prompted by more than one reason. There is nothing necessarily wrong with that. It can be quite efficient to keep two birds in one basket and to satisfy two motives with the same behavior. One theme of this book is the mutual benefit that can come about in supportive relationships. Thus, behavior can be motivated by both the desire to give and the desire to receive. Difficulties happen when there is defensiveness or lack of clarity about what motives are operating.

Recently I asked a colleague for some information. She told me: "Sure, no trouble. I have to go through those old files anyway to get something for myself." I felt some relief that I could get what I needed without undue hardship on her. Her honesty in this respect also gave me evidence that she will tell me if I later make a request she considers unreasonable. Is the help less helpful to me because she had some personal gains from her action? Do you not get the groceries you need when you are sick if I do some of my own grocery shopping while I'm doing yours? There is still a gift. My friend had to keep my need as well as her own in mind in going through the files. I looked for your groceries as well as my own.

Without such clarity, the recipient may feel more in debt than need be, and the donor may claim more glory than is realistic. If I claim to go to the grocery store only for you, I am misleading you and myself. I build up a false image of myself as a person whose only concern is to serve. It is tempting to ignore the other reasons that might be uncomfortable to admit. Getting groceries for you might satisfy my nosiness about your life or be a good excuse for getting out of some unpleasant work I need to do. *I* will have to pay the price of my self-deception. *You* might as well! False images have to be defended. Defending false images means wasted energy. The image of being a "good" and nurturing person can keep us from being one.

RULES AND CHOICES

WHEN "BEING GOOD" IS IMPORTANT

A general motive is to be "a good person," including being supportive, helpful, and nurturing. This can also be called a value. Curiously, the more important the value or motive, the easier it is to be misled. Because being good and nurturing is so important, we are likely to have many defenses to protect our Glorious Image as a good and nurturing person. As part of this, we probably have many internal voices reminding us of what is good: "Lend a helping hand." "Don't be selfish." "Give to the poor." "Visit the sick and those in prison." The result is that most of us are *less* moral in our behavior than we want to be, and less so than we could be. The problem is assuming the voices to be our own and concluding that, therefore, we are moral, upright, proper, nurturing. If your experiences in the world have been fairly typical, some questioning may be in order. Whose voice is that? Is it really your own voice? Why do you want to help?

False Security. "I know I'm a good and nurturing person because when I hear of someone's trouble, I want to help." That easy acceptance of "I want to" can be an indication that the idea is a security blanket: we can rest secure that we are moral and upright (somewhat like the "Of Course I Am!" person). True, we offer help when emergencies are called to our attention. But how many emergencies could we have helped to *avoid* if we had been more concerned? Needs for support come in many forms. They do not always merit newspaper headlines or a special call on the phone or mention from the pulpit. Being a truly nurturing person is a way of life, being continually alert to people and their needs. Some people are foul-weather friends—they are there when times are tough but they do not help to prevent the tough times.

They are valuable as foul-weather friends, but how much more valuable they would be if they were fair-weather friends as well. Mary is full of sympathy and support when there is a big problem, but is never around during the ordinary times when small problems build up to the big ones. When Leah was critically ill, her hospital room was full of flowers and visitors. She was comforted by the concern shown for her—there is value in attention in emergencies. However, when she came home and faced the long hard work of rehabilitation, she found that the novelty and drama of her needs had worn off for many people, and their sudden care had been only a flash in the pan. She felt that she had been only a "special call" who was not valued for herself. Her task of nurturing herself was made extra hard because she was confused about the automatic care that people had given and then withdrawn.

Automatic Actions. With the security blanket, nurture becomes automatic. That may sound ideal—being a good person without even trying! The danger is that the behavior is without personal involvement, so the person is not a person, but an Efficient Robot or a Fulfilled Tape Recorder. Several years ago one of my students expected refusal of his request to take an exam early, though he had a very good reason. I surprised him by saying, "Of course." He praised me for being such a fair person. Before he got out the door, I realized that I had no memory of what he had just told me about his problem. I had acted only from habit, or from the "top layer" of my head. Although I knew I'd made the decision I should have, by my own values, I felt uncomfortable. A robot could have done what I had done. The robot also could go haywire without my noticing! Certainly, I felt guilty accepting the praise he gave me. Yes, there are limits to how much personal caring energy I can give. But if I am to be a nurturing person, I cannot be a creature of automatic habits.

"I SHOULD"

Stars for the Crown. If you have had somewhat typical experiences, your nurture is probably led and misled by a lot of "shoulds" that are really the voices of other people telling you who you must be if you are to be lovable and acceptable to them. In hearing and obeying the shoulds, we feel moral and lovable, with hope of escaping punishment and receiving rewards. We expect stars of the love and praise of other people or stars for a crown in a later life. Working for stars means that the *glory* of being a good person is more important than *being* a good person. When that glory is the aim, one is not really a good person. If we're thinking of the rewards for nurturing, we're distracted from the task of nurturing. We may drift into automatic habits or become a Suffering Servant or a "See Me" person, for example. If we really believe in nurture, we will not be a friend who rushes in only when there is extreme need and we can gain glory in the drama. We must focus on the task at hand instead of on rewards. With mature adult love, we give even when we do not get credit.

The pressure of shoulds and the lure of the stars can lead to deeds that need doing, when otherwise they might not get done! Remember, behavior can be helpful, whatever the motives. When we are not sure what we are about in the game of life, the shoulds given by others can be very helpful in offering guidance, and the stars can be a useful incentive or goad to action. Yet the role of shoulds and stars is to serve as a diving board into mature involvement in and responsibility for our own lives. The child who is lured by the stars of other people's approval, or glories after this life, needs to be transformed into an adult. Conforming to the rules of other people for the sake of the rewards they offer is not adult moral behavior.

Personal Responsibility and Involvement. What is left out in following the shoulds given by others is our own personal creative powers and our own responsibility for involvement with life. No amount of following rules can make up for that. The widow made a personal decision to give something very precious in her life—a mite. Are we all to follow the example and give a mite? It is the principle that is important. A mite for one person might be five dollars, and for another five thousand dollars. In many cases, a gift of time and personal energy instead of money can be as big as the widow's mite. How is the principle to be enacted in the life of a particular person? Each person is responsible for answering. The answer requires not shoulds taken in from others but personal involvement in one's own life along with responsibility for the talents of one's life. Only I have the gift of *my* life. Only I can give that from that. A gift made from habit or fear instead of from my own personness is superficial. The superficial acceptance of the voices of others telling us what we "want to" do and "should" do is really a way of avoiding adult responsibility for our own commitment to life, including a dedication to use our own creative capacities. Listening only to the voices of others is a way of being a robot, and being childish rather than adult.

CHOICE WITHIN A PERSONAL PROFESSION

We can easily get overwhelmed in the process of trying to give to others, while avoiding self-deception or wasted energy, or computer-like uninvolvement in obeying rules. The confusion can be lessened, though not completely avoided, by shifting our thinking of ourselves in a couple of ways.

Choice. The first way is to think of ourselves as choosers. Many of the problems that people tumble into without knowing what happened arise because they are not aware of their right and responsibility to choose and, in fact, do not choose consciously. When people are aware of choice, they feel better and do better. When we are aware of a choice, we consider the situation and ourselves more carefully and thoroughly than otherwise. In that process we become more personally involved. As we choose, we make a commitment of ourselves to the seriousness of the action. There is a big difference between my feeding a friend's cat or my visiting at the hospital because I think, "I should," and because I think, "This is my choice, a part of what I choose to be." On a rainy Saturday afternoon when I have a lot of work to do, I may have to kick myself with a few shoulds. But they are shoulds I choose to follow because of who I choose to be. The shoulds may be of the same content as those I have been taught, but following them is more joyous when I remember to choose.

The Second Mile. Choosing to walk the second mile is very different from feeling you have to—you should!— walk the first. As long as you do only what is required of you, you are a slave. The moment you do one bit more, you are a free person. In fact, choosing to do that one bit more that is not required often can help remind us that we do have a choice about the supposedly required *first* mile. For example, I asked Ann to bring me groceries when I was sick. She brought me a bouquet of fresh daisies as well. The flowers perked me up. The fact that she brought them helped me to know she really was glad to bring the needed groceries—I felt more nurtured than I would have with groceries but no daisies. Similarly, sometimes I am fretful at an ill-timed visit or call. At such times, I listen with the strained patience of resentment, which is not hidden as well as I think. When I can relax into myself enough to ask for more information or to bring up another thing to talk about, I am reminded that I did not have to accept the visit or call. I feel more free and more engaged in what is happening. In offering the second mile, I am being *me* in the interaction rather than a victim of the circumstances.

Also, we may be more helpful in the second mile than in the first. Remember that people often are hesitant to ask for what they want or in many instances do not know their real desires. After the anxious first mile is over, they may feel more comfortable saying what is really on their minds. When they are not clear for themselves, the walk during the second mile can provide the occasion for them to stumble upon their real needs. You may, "just trying to make conversation," in that freely chosen second mile, make a helpful suggestion. Sometimes what they need is for you to offer that extra walk.

An Honorable Profession. The second way of seeing ourselves is to see our nurture as part of our chosen profession of ministry. Some people are paid by society for the professional helping services they provide with the care and skill they have developed over long years. Generally, a minister is one who supplies something needed. Two themes of this book are that we need to give and receive nurture, and that each person can develop the skills and attitude of nurture, which requires much work. Thus the profession of being a nurturing minister is there to be accepted. I have no choice about what human beings are or how we are made. I have no choice about what seems to me the fact that effective human living requires relating to others in mature, productive love. However, I do have the choice to accept that or to try to turn my back on it. I do have a choice about what I will do in *my* life to meet *my* own obligations to fulfill human nature in *myself.* The work of nurture deserves the dignity of being considered a profession and a ministry. Losing sight of this big picture usually is accompanied by depressions and ineffectiveness. As "just a person," it is easy to give in to being a nosy do-gooder, or trying to be important, for example. Remembering the big picture of my profession as a nurturer helps me to get up on a wintry morning and manage to get about with the business of the day with more effectiveness and enjoyment than if I forget. In chapters to follow, attention will be given to some of the practicalities of work as a nurturer.

CHAPTER 5

Now What Do I Do?— How to Support

There are no simple rules about support in all situations, but there are some basic features of nurturing that are often overlooked. A small investment of attention in these ways can bring many rewards. Listening, honest sharing, and clear praise are the topics of this chapter. In the next chapter, we will look at making choices about whom to support. Knowing your motives and loving yourself are necessary.

STARTING WITH WHAT YOU HAVE—YOU!

To nurture well, start with what you have. You are the source of your nurture, and the best gift you can give is yourself. Some people are simply nice to be around, even though they are "just ordinary people." Being with them is therapeutic—you feel better about yourself and the world. How do they do that? If you ask them what they do, they would probably say something like, "Oh, nothing special, I'm just being myself." That's the important point, just being yourself, spontaneously and honestly, with active involvement in what is going on around you. Many people, however, cannot or will not do that. They may have mixed or hidden motives they are not clear about, lack of self-love and personal anchoring, or rigid habits and ways of relating to people. Basically they do not really love and value themselves. How can you give to others by being yourself if you do not know and love yourself? To feel free and confident enough to let go and be yourself, you must take yourself seriously—know and value yourself.

Ironically, many women feel that they exist only to give. At the same time, they have a very low opinion of themselves and of what they can give. Thus, they work extra hard at giving to make up for what they think are their lacks. They might be Busybody Bumblebees, Superwomen, or dependent workaholics. Many other women are not so extreme, but still do not realistically value themselves and what they have to give. You may not think you have much to give, while others have much. Perhaps you are more aware of what others *could* give you but do not. Perhaps the other people feel the same, thinking they have nothing to offer while you have much! People often take themselves for granted, just as they take nurture for granted.

Don't hide your light. You probably have a great deal of common sense and sensitivity built up through many experiences in life. You also have your own unique interests, insights, and talents. Even when people see their talents, they often feel they should not let others know that. While we are told to avoid thinking more highly of ourselves than we ought, we are *not* told to think more "lowly" of ourselves than we ought. A light should not be put under a basket. If you hide your light, or turn a spotlight only on your weaknesses, other people cannot ask you to share your strengths with them. If you value yourself, take yourself seriously and listen to yourself, it is easier to value others, to take them seriously and listen to them.

THE GIFT OF LISTENING

HARD WORK

A gift that people often need most and do not get is someone really to listen. Most people do not do the hard work necessary to listen well. They listen only passively. They are not free of their own concerns enough to hear what the other person is really expressing. In passive, superficial listening, the words flow in one ear and out the other. They may stay only long enough to trigger an action, as in the example of my not hearing a student's problem. They may stay in the head long enough for a "carbon copy" to be made. But accurate recording of details is no guarantee that real listening has taken place. A tape recorder could do that. Surely there have been times when your saying "But you said . . ." has been followed by their saying, "But that's not what I was talking about." You missed the message even though the words all "registered."

Being Involved in Listening. Real listening is more like a psychological meeting of "souls" or psyches than a recording. That requires active involvement in order to feel what the other person is feeling. Experience is shared. To do this, listeners need a well-founded self-trust and self-anchoring. Otherwise, they lose themselves or cannot really hear. According to the famous psychologist Carl Rogers, to understand the messages of other people we need to see *as if* from their perspective or frame of reference. The aims are, first, to see from their viewpoint while not losing our own and, second, to keep hold on our own views while not imposing them on the other. We can't really understand a person unless we walk a day in that person's shoes. Rogers said that the real trick is walking in two pairs of shoes at the same time—the other person's and our own—and keeping track of which is which! That is not easy at best.

Sometimes people are too eager to understand, and thus make the mistake of letting go of their own frame of reference too much. They respond only to the other's views and thereby lose themselves. Probably more people make the opposite mistake, out of fear of making the first. Real listening is scary! They hold back from real listening out of fear that they will lose their own centering. They may become dogmatic and glue on their shoes, just to be sure, or try to get you to exchange your shoes for theirs. You can sometimes see this in somebody's being too quick to talk or talking in the wrong way.

Too Quick to Talk. It is amazing how often people confuse listening with talking. The false logic seems to be something like: "If I really hear, I will have a lot to say. So, the more I talk, the better I have heard." Their aim in listening is only to find an excuse to talk. Such people are talkative Busybody Bumblebees. They talk so much they are bound to hit on something relevant at some point, but this is happenstance more than a sign of real listening. They may explain their lack of listening (a fault) as trying to help (a virtue).

For example, Fran often does not wait to find out what the other person wants or already knows. In response to a comment such as, "I'm thinking of changing the kitchen floor," she might launch into a five-minute speech on how to install the kind of flooring she just put in. What she does not give the other person a chance to say is, "But I have to use the money to fix the car instead," or, "My cousin has arranged to have what I want done at dealer's cost." The five minutes about Fran's floor could have been spent better talking about her knowledge about car repair shops, or sharing delight about the helpful cousin. Fran adds to difficulties instead of helping. Her attitude is: "I have all the answers. You have none." The listener is frustrated or confused: "Why does she think she has to take charge of my kitchen floor!" or, "It seems more important to her to tell me about her new floor than to hear about my old car."

Talking at *Someone—"You should..."* Fran is too quick to talk, and to talk *at*. People who talk less can be doing the same. They give advice but not the comfort of contact. They judge rather than listen, giving pronouncements or sermons: "You should do this," "You should not have done that." Fran's basic message was, "You should do what I did." It is much easier to talk *at* a person than with a person, to judge rather than to understand. The judging can be shown in many ways. "You're busy and didn't have time" can show that the speaker understands the situation you are in so that the house is still a mess or the letter still not written. It can also be said in such a way that you feel that the pressures of your situation are being dismissed as unimportant and you are being judged negatively: "You should have, no matter what; you are careless and thoughtless"; or, "I really don't care what you've been through." The listener is concerned with the mess or the letter more than with you. A look or tone of voice can also show the judgment. "Why are you upset by that?" can be a judgment that "You should not be upset by that," rather than a statement of concern and an invitation for you to talk. In such ways, the benefits of listening are held back.

SOME BENEFITS TO BE GAINED BY LISTENING

Permission to Feel What You Are Feeling. What do you want when you talk something over with someone? Much of what you want cannot be given by people who talk *at* you, judging you rather than understanding you. Trusting the listener to "be with you" instead of judging you is particularly important when the issue has to do with feelings. Feelings just *are,* and are to be accepted as that. Ideally, we should know and accept ourselves enough to know what we are feeling. But there are problems. Many feelings are not well accepted and often are judged or explained away. We do that too much to ourselves with defenses and protective illusions. We do not need a friend to do it to us as well.

It takes a person comfortable with her own feelings to be able to accept someone else's feelings. Such a person can give "permission" to go ahead and feel what we are feeling, and help give clarity about exactly what the feelings are. There may be two kinds of feelings mixed together in a blur, such as gladness for someone along with anger or jealousy, or relief along with disappointment. There may be a feeling we are hesitant to admit to ourselves, such as anger at a loved one or anxiety about our own welfare. People may have trouble admitting such feelings because they are carrying around big shoulds: "I should not be angry at someone I love," or, "I should be thinking about someone else instead of myself." Shoulds get us into a lot of trouble! We often talk judgmentally at ourselves instead of really listening to ourselves. We criticize ourselves instead of trying to understand ourselves. Thus, we do not nurture ourselves and are less able to nurture others. A nurturing friend can help correct that situation.

A third party can help us accept ourselves and offer another perspective. Someone else telling us "it's okay" to have feelings, irrational and confusing as they are, can do wonders. Another person has more freedom to say: "In that situation, I'd be glad for her, of course, but I'd also be really furious about how it happened!" or, "I know you're concerned about him, but you need to take care of yourself, too!" Such comments can help us to see our anger or self-concern. They can give assurance: "I'm not really a bad person or crazy for feeling what I feel. . . . I'm okay."

Discovering Answers Ourselves. Just as we get confused about feelings, we can get confused about other life issues and lose perspective (though in truth, confusions about other issues often involve confusions about feelings). The solutions to the major crises of life and to the minor ones we think are major often are within us. We just need some help in trusting ourselves so that we can get to them. Nurturing listeners do not necessarily have the answers. Instead, by really listening, they set the stage on which we can accept and trust ourselves and find "the answer" ourselves. Also, telling someone else of the situation can help us see a detail, or a possibility, or a perspective that we missed previously. A simple obvious question from someone who is trying to understand can help us "break set" and get out of a rut in thinking. I have been thanked and thanked too often to count, when a solution was suddenly discovered, with the "helper" doing nothing other than listening. The helper has, nonetheless, helped by being there to hear, without judgment.

In some situations, the helper is seen as one who can and will help by giving answers. That leads to hope that there is a solution to the problem. With the hope, and reduced worry about being helpless, it is easier to discover the solution yourself. Making the decision to talk with someone about a problem can "release" the solution for the same reason. Thus, it is helpful just knowing that a sympathetic ear is available, even before you talk into that ear. People who judgmentally talk at a person do not provide such an ear.

Seeing the Problems. The help a real listener gives can be to point out a problem. From a distance, another person can see that there are problems and what they are. For example, trivial things or big issues can mount up too quickly or too gradually—with the result that people do not stop to realize the total effect of what is happening to them. Having someone point out the stress can be helpful. Many of my friends complain and beat themselves psychologically because they feel depressed and incompetent: "I just can't seem to get on top of things." My usual response is something like: "Stop beating yourself. Look at all you've been going through. No wonder you feel tired!"

One friend was adjusting to divorce, having trouble with house payments after having had to buy a new house, and faced with a twelve-year-old car breaking down. She could not understand why she felt so incompetent and why she broke down "just because" the bathtub drain stopped up. A luxurious bath was a joyful gift she gave herself every morning, so she felt petty and guilty being upset by such a thing! In ordinary situations, she would have been very annoyed at the bathroom drain, but it would not have been the focus for self-blame that it became.

The "treatment" of pointing out stress does not remove the stress. It does, however, help people stop using energy in feeling confused and bad about themselves. Also, it often gives people a bit of pride at their coping abilities: "Considering everything that's happened, I'm really doing well. I'm not so bad after all!" That itself provides more energy and optimism for dealing with the problems. Once the confidence and hope are aroused, it is easier to see ways to deal with the problems. We could, of course, do much the same for ourselves. A nurturing listener can help us do what we do not do for ourselves. In turn, the more we can listen to ourselves, the more we can listen to and really share with others.

THE GIFT OF HONEST SHARING

SELF-DISCLOSURE

Real listening to the concerns, joys, and problems of other people is hard work. So, too, is real sharing of our own concerns, joys, and problems. Like listening, sharing requires a lot of self-trust and is an important gift to others. Social courtesy can become a bad habit—"How are you?" is followed immediately with, "I'm fine, too, thank you," without hearing the other person's response or daring to admit, "Things are lousy." Much of what people share in discussion with one another is superficial chitchat or misinformed gossip about other people. The real sharing of disclosing ourselves to another person involves daring to be real with ourselves and with another. What many people share often is misleadingly positive, as illustrated by the idea of the Christmas letter.

THE CHRISTMAS LETTER SYNDROME

Some Christmas letters are very honest, warm, sharing statements. Yet the Christmas letter stands as a dominant cultural symbol of mentioning only the positive, often with a bragging of superficial accomplishments. The picture given is of the "happy little family": Wife got a B+ on a philosophy term paper; Junior was elected vice-president of the stamp club; husband was invited to join the Junior Chamber of Commerce; daughter was runner-up for the second squad of the softball team. Why not show how these successes are important to the family that is sending the letter? If I am a real friend, I can understand disappointments over the C− papers, or the children's previous problems of adapting to a new school. Real sharing is likely to include some hurts and failures as well as happinesses and successes.

Reduced Self-Esteem in Comparison. Superficial suc-

cess stories have disadvantages for both the persons who
give them and the persons who hear them. When others
show us only their successful side, it is easy to assume
that everyone else is a success in life: "Only my family
and I have problems." We need information from and
about other people to understand ourselves. Emphasis
on only the superficially positive is dishonest and misleading. It reduces self-esteem and blocks getting to
know people. If you have been overwhelmed by success
stories, nurture yourself by remembering your own
strengths and the probable defensiveness of people who
claim success only. When we are feeling weak and
vulnerable, it is hard not to feel more weak and useless
hearing about the seemingly unlimited happiness of
others.

Reduced Help with Reduced Honesty. There are disadvantages also for the people who reveal only the positive
side. It is hard to relate to people who are "just too good
to be true." It is hard to be excited about a step forward if
we think those people do nothing but step forward,
without the slides backward we know we have. We can
better share their joys if we know of their frustrations as
well. Also, a basic way of asking for help is simply to
reveal yourself as a person. If you show only strengths
and happiness, success, and self-sufficiency, others do
not see the need to offer nurture. Thus, they are less
likely to detect clues to the need for nurture, and less
likely to offer support. Or, if you do ask for support, they
may underestimate or overestimate your need because
you so seldom mention problems: "Oh, she's so strong,
she didn't really mean it, she'll get on top of this." Or,
"Oh my goodness, if it's enough for her to mention, it
must really be a problem!"

In sum, showing other people your weaknesses and
vulnerabilities can be a way of giving. Giving an "honest" picture of the way things are gives honest informa-

tion about life for people to use in evaluating themselves. It also gives others the opportunity to be strong for you. If it is important to you to nurture others, perhaps it is important to them to nurture you. Hiding behind images of continual success, happiness, and self-sufficiency inhibits their giving. Receiving their strength can be a way of giving to them.

GIVING THANKS AND PRAISE

USING WORDS TO HELP

There is an awful lot of living that goes into life! So much of the big picture is made up of details, of who made the coffee or took the garbage out, who said what when and found something positive to say when a person was being criticized, or who remembered to say thank you. The big picture matters, such as who comes through in a tough situation. But the small details—not really so small—matter as well. Among those small details are what we say when and how we say it. The subtle nuances may be "just a matter of words," but they may say much about the big picture of caring. We need to watch our words and actions otherwise as much as we watch our intent and attitude.

People often neglect the obvious thing of telling other people that they are valued. My amazement about other people on this score is surpassed only by my amazement at myself for doing the same thing. We can value a person tremendously but, somehow, never let the person know that directly. Yes, our value may be shown in the deep "ways that really count." However, those continuingly important ways can also be rather abstract. In the midst of the hustle and bustle of life, it is easy to wonder whether friends are just taking you for granted. A special effort with a telephone call just to say thanks, or an unexpected friendship card or little gift can do wonders.

There is less wondering whether the compliment was the superficial courtesy of "just being nice" if you make a special attempt, or at least bring up the topic of your appreciation of the friend.

Specific Feedback. Another way to have the thanks or praise be taken seriously is to make it specific. Specific praise also gives more information to the other person. How often have you been confused because someone praised you? You felt good, but were not really sure what you did right, or what you did that was any different from usual. As far as you could tell, you led the meeting as you always do, or followed the same old recipe in making the cake. In such situations, I am pleased by the compliment, but my delight is quickly replaced by confusion and some fear. If I don't know what I did to make it a good job this time, they'll expect a good job from me next time and I won't know what to do! Specific feedback usually is clear and useful.

You may know that you highly value your friend's humor, insight, knowledge, or common sense. You may know that everyone else does too. It may seem so obvious to you that you never realize that your friend does not realize that she has those traits and that she is valued for being herself. By telling her, you increase her information about herself and increase her sense of self-worth and being valued as well.

RESPONSIBILITY TO CARE, TO SEE, TO SAY

For praise to be most effective, it must be honest. That requires hard work, just as does real listening, to see what deserves praise. Giving specific feedback involves a responsibility to know what we see and value. What is it about the meeting or the cake that we really noticed this time? Why are we glad the friend watered the plants? Is it really for the sake of the plants themselves? Or is that we like knowing that a friend is willing to do it?

The really important part about help in practical ways often is the emotional support it shows. To nurture other people well, we need to care enough to notice what they do and how they do it. We need to know what we value as well. There is no substitute for knowledge and love, of self and others. This is true also in making decisions about whom to support, as will be discussed in the next chapter.

CHAPTER 6

Whom to Support When and How

Nurturing others and oneself has many rewards of giving and growing. Making choices can increase the harvest of rewards for one's self and others. How can we use nurturing energy most effectively, for the greatest good? Both the giver and the receiver must assume their rights and responsibilities of choosing. Making good decisions requires knowing and valuing yourself as well as others.

DECISIONS ABOUT GIVING AND RECEIVING

THE FACT OF CHOICE IN GIVING

People think carefully about how to use their money, but they are not always so careful with their time, energy, and love. Your nurture is a valuable gift to be invested wisely and made to grow. With this attitude, it is easier to see opportunities for nurture and growth. To take an extreme example: if someone you love is seriously ill, you can moan and groan or you can look for something to do. What strengths do you have ready to be used? What strengths can the situation encourage you to develop? Choosing requires paying attention to yourself and being personally involved, as discussed in a previous chapter.

Without choosing, you may not give what you could or you may try to give too much. Stop and think is a good rule. Decision-making can also free you for giving with confidence and joy, with a value on what you give and zest in giving it.

Give with Joy. Some people do not give what they could because they do not realize what they have to offer or they underestimate its value. Other people give timidly and without joy because they themselves do not value what they have to offer. They are apologetic for their offerings. Still others give only from a sense of "having to" and external "oughts." "Be a cheerful giver" is usually said as criticism to those who feel resentful about being obliged to give. I have caught myself agreeing to take a friend on an errand and then being grumpy the whole time. I have said yes out of habit, without thinking and choosing. The joy is missing. If you offer to do something for a friend, relax and let yourself enjoy it. If you cannot enjoy a task, think twice about choosing to do it. Choosing requires paying attention to yourself. Thus, you can mean what you say and say what you mean.

TOO EAGER TO GIVE

Realism: Superwoman You're Not! Responsible choosing means knowing the reasons for your actions. What are your motives in offering nurture? To show love for others, or to win love for yourself? With lack of self-love or self-knowledge, you are likely to be too eager to give and attempt to give what you cannot. Many women unrealistically attempt to be all things to all people. They may be just caught in a rut of the habit of giving. They may be attempting to convince themselves and others that they are lovable and worthy. They reduce the quality, and ultimately the quantity, of their nurture by attempting to meet too many needs of others and too few of their own. In addition, some women have unrealistically high standards for whatever they do. Superwoman wants to be a gourmet cook of local renown, and to have the top job in her profession in three years. The house must be an immaculate showplace, not merely clean enough to live in. A hobby is not for fun, but another demand for excellence. Everything she does must be admired as extraordinary. She may be a workaholic or dependent on the admiration of others.

Anybody's time and energy are limited. What are the things most important to you? Make realistic decisions in the light of who you are and how you want to grow. Choosing "just getting by" in some domains can be realistic and growthful, and can free energy for the things that really matter.

What Does the Other Person Want? In eagerness, people can miss hearing what the other says and so talk *at* or not give what is wanted. Although going the second mile has advantages, there can be too much of a good thing, particularly if you have not really listened. The effect can be to make the receivers feel that their own wishes and feelings have been ignored. When her folks asked her what she wanted for her birthday, Betty chose a toaster because her husband was never really pleased with her early-morning efforts at making toast in the oven. So her parents gave her an expensive portable oven, and she still had the problem of fixing toast. She also had the frustration of feeling guilty about her anger and being disappointed because they did not really listen to her when she explained what she wanted.

Deliver What You Offer. In eagerness to give, it is easy also to offer more than you are willing to deliver, and to give without letting the other person have a say-so. Mean what you say, and follow through. One friend repeatedly offers to come early to help with party preparations, and to bring some special cooking utensil. She usually is the last guest to arrive, showing no awareness of the chaos caused by the missing pot. Ruth has caused even more confusion than this. She decided that Nan's bedroom floor needed resanding. Before Nan could think about Ruth's offer to do it, Ruth was moving the furniture out of the room. Ruth left after the room was empty (and other rooms overly full!), saying she would be back the next day to do the floor. With daily promises for the next day, Nan endured the resulting disorder rather than risk insulting Ruth, who was doing her such a favor. Finally, she gave up and restored order, without new floors. Ruth still sticks her head in the bedroom and tsk-tsks about the floors. Offer what you know you can give, and give with confidence and joy what you offer.

Plans for Yourself. A good test of whether you really feel choice or are too eager to give is whether or not you are willing to say no to someone else because of your own preferences, including plans for yourself. Many people need to practice saying no. If you are not free to say no, then your yes does not mean as much as it could, and other people can take advantage of you without your realizing it. You do not have to explain your reasons, though you can indicate your openness by saying something in addition to no. "What! Let you drive my new car!" is very different from, "Well, I'm not really comfortable lending you my new car, but I'll be glad to drive you there if we can arrange a good time." "If it has to be done on Wednesday, I can't help, but I could Tuesday or Thursday."

You have a right to refuse for any reason, including having plans for yourself. People are particularly hesitant to assume a choice to refuse a request or an offer if they have no plans with someone else. There seems to be a "cultural rule" that everyone would prefer to be with someone than to be alone. Being alone is seen as "doing nothing" and doing anything is better than doing nothing. People who assume that are not taking themselves

seriously. Sometimes I know that a friend will understand when I say I know I will be too tired to come to a
party two weeks away. For other people, I must use
generalities: "I have plans." It is not a lie. I do have
plans for a quiet evening I need. We must feel free to say
yes to ourselves and no to other people if we are to know
and to nurture ourselves and improve our nurture of
others.

RECEIVER'S DECISIONS AND RESPONSIBILITIES

The cultural pressure to "be nice and give" encourages overlooking the basic fact that the potential receiver
has responsibilities and rights, just as does the giver.
Without the recognition of the receiver's right of choice,
the other person is reduced to an object. Without responsibility shared by the receiver, the gifts can be misused.

The Right to Say No. The right of choice is brought out
strongly by the right of refusal for either person. It is your
right to refuse to give what the other wants. It is the other
person's right not to need or not to elect to accept
supportive actions offered. People do sometimes have
trouble saying, "No, thank you," just as they have trouble
saying, "Yes, thank you." When the no is said, it may not
be accepted, particularly if the giver has mixed motives
in giving. A kind friend once announced to me that she
was going to give me a party on a day that was important
to me, and had already started arranging with other
people. Apparently she thought I was just being overly
humble when I said I did not want that. She proceeded
with even more elaborate plans. I tossed and turned
several nights. How could I be so ungrateful as to refuse!
After all, she was being thoughtful. At the same time, I
felt resentful that she was giving me no right to express
myself. I felt guilt about wanting to refuse, *and* about not
refusing. I thought I arrived at a suitable compromise,
expressing my appreciation for her thoughtfulness while

allowing me some of what I wanted for the day. It is not clear that she has forgiven me for not going along with her plans. Should I have accepted in spite of my own preferences? She was kind enough to offer. On the other hand, does a person lose all rights of choice just because someone else wants to be generous?

If You Don't Ask, Don't Complain! People who want to receive nurture must take the responsibility of showing their need and accepting the help offered. Let caring others know of your need and accept their nurture, or forfeit your right to complain. Other people have no way of knowing your need if you do not tell them. I once felt very resentful that a friend did not offer to help when I was sick. Later, she rightly pointed out that I had told her that the medicine prescribed was supposed to clear up the problem. I neglected to mention that the problem would get worse for the couple of days necessary for the medicine to take effect. In many other situations as well, people can be unclear about their needs.

When an offer is made, clearly accept or refuse. The example was given in Chapter 3 of a woman who three times declined an offer she wanted to accept, and then felt let down when I did not give in spite of her refusals. She could not admit that she was not completely self-sufficient and wanted help. Other people would rather complain about lack of support than receive it. Becky complains that she has no supportive friends. Yet when someone offers help with a job, she makes no response. Suggesting a firm plan is criticized as an attempt to control her. So the person offering help drops the issue. The result is criticism for not helping her.

Taking More than Is Offered. Part of the receiver's responsibility is to know and to communicate clearly what is wanted, and not to try to take more. I offered quite happily to take a friend to the grocery store. What she did not tell me was that to her, grocery shopping meant driving all over town to take advantage of the different bargains at each big store. The afternoon disappeared bit by bit as I kept telling myself, "Oh, one more stop won't matter." She should have made clear what she was asking. I also should have made sure I knew what she was asking. In contrast, when Kate was moving, she was quite clear. With each person, she arranged a specific task or a specific time for helping. Her friends knew what she expected, and Kate tried to take no more. She got what she needed, without taking advantage of anyone. That required thoughtful planning and consideration for other people.

A "No" Answer. Some people are too quick to ask for and to accept help. Sometimes nurture means saying no, refusing a request for support. Easier said than done! Carol emphasizes her problems. Friends rush to the rescue: "Poor dear, everything goes wrong for her, I'll help." However, the sympathy and help she receives encourage her to keep asking for help. She does not use the nurture given to her for growthful purposes. Other people let her get away with it. They need to say, perhaps, "No, use what you've already been given."

MATCHING ISSUES

Comfortable nurturing relationships require effective choosing on the part of each person. Part of the choosing is about the match of two persons. What can be expected with any particular person? What can you share and how can you grow with a particular person? What do you have to give and choose to give? What does the other person want from you? What does the other offer you? The content and extent of matching vary tremendously, from matching in limited and tangible ways to deeper and more abstract ones.

WHO, WHEN, AND WHAT?

Practicalities of Circumstance. Relationships are affected by practical factors that bring two persons to the same place at the same time, such as geography, schedules, and interests. We do not have direct control over who moves in next door or who goes to the meeting we do. Thus, we may develop meaningful friendships with persons we would not have thought of seeking out: "It just worked out nicely." On the other hand, we may not develop or maintain desired relationships because the "accidents" of our lives discourage that. If we do not stop to think, choice is taken from us as circumstances take over. When Vicky moved to the other side of town, we both kept putting off using the extra energy needed to get together. Now we both regret that we let "just circumstance" take over.

In contrast, my friendship with Jill did not last long after her children came back from summer vacation because she was never free in the evenings until she had put them to bed and cleaned the house. At that time, I had to go to bed at about the same time as her children! Her children are older now, and my work schedule has changed, but Jill and I have drifted apart because of "circumstance." The relationship we had is no less valuable because of its short duration. Sometimes there is just not a good match, or the match does not last over time: "It wasn't meant to be." That does not necessarily mean that there is anything wrong. Neither person needs to feel put out or put down, though often each does. What and who make a good match can vary with the practicalities of one's current life.

Circumstances sometimes seem to pit one person against another. "Make new friends, but keep the old; the new are silver, the old are gold" is good advice but can be difficult to put into practice. An important commitment to one friend may interfere with having the time or energy to develop a friendship with another person. Some people get so excited about newly discovered silver friends that they drop the golden older friends. Others cling to the old so tightly that they do not seek new friends and may stifle their own growth and that of their friends. If you want both the silver and the gold, there must be clear decision-making and communication. Whether a relationship lasts through practical difficulties depends in part on the importance each person assigns to the relationship. With awareness of limited time and energy, thoughtful planning and clear thinking through of what you want with other people is important.

The Value of Limited Matches. Decision-making also involves knowing and accepting the limits on the relationship. A supportive enjoyable relationship need not cover all aspects of one's life, nor need it last a lifetime or even a few years. Because of interests and schedules, one person may be a good match for Saturday afternoon movies, but not for Saturday afternoon bridge games or Saturday night concerts. Personality styles are relevant. Millie was very competitive, and Mary was very conceited. Their competitiveness and conceit were challenging and meaningful to each other in the setting of tennis, but not otherwise. They enjoyed their weekly tennis game together. Before and after the game, they could have nice talks. When they tried to see each other in other contexts, one (or both!) ended up complaining to me about the other. The relationship was a limited one, but still of value and importance to each when the limitation was accepted.

I call one friend when I feel playful and another when I feel stupid and weak. When I need supporting discussion about religious issues, some people cannot give that to me. Others can give then but cannot give when it's women's issues that are on my mind. Still others are comfortable only if we talk about our shared work interests and our pets. The limited relationships in which I can be only part of what I am are valuable. However, I must be clear with myself on who I am and what I want and can expect from each different person.

Expecting Too Much from One Person. The value of limited relationships often is overlooked and not developed. This probably has been one of the prices we pay because this society generally does not value nurturing relationships between adults not in the family. Marriage and family relationships are often assumed to be the only ones that really matter, with all needs met through them. This assumption usually is unrealistic and puts quite a pressure on the family. Even when looking outside of traditional marriage, we are led to "all or nothing" thinking—meaning that if one need is met or one kind of interest shared, we tend to assume that all can be. There is a tendency to expect too much from any one person. For example, when people are brought together by circumstance, they may expect too much of each other simply because they are around each other a lot. They may try to develop the relationship beyond its natural match, thinking it is more than it is. In friendships or work relationships, a person who meets some needs can be discovered as not able or willing to meet all needs. The discovery often causes unrealistic appraisal of the relationship: "I thought I could count on you!" "I must have been wrong about you and the relationship." The expectation is unrealistic, as is the response when the expectation is not fulfilled.

Respecting the Unmet Needs and the Mistakes. People sometimes are unrealistic in expecting a perfect match on all relevant factors, and unrealistic when their expectations are not met. One unrealistic response is to deprecate or put down the needs that are not shared or satisfied in the relationship, considering them as not being worthy of attention. For example, Rebecca insists that everything be very "up" and cheerfully optimistic. When her friends are feeling heavy examining some of the deeper issues of life, she attempts to lighten their mood. She can provide a needed uplift. But if the friend has to insist on continuing with "serious thoughts," Rebecca criticizes or disappears. The need the friend states is discounted as not important. Rebecca does not respect the needs she cannot meet and does not share.

A related way of not taking another person's need seriously is to dismiss it as a mistake. It was very important to Gail to gain acceptance to a particular group. The only reasons her friend Jan could see for Gail's intense concern were childishly superficial. Gail felt let down. There are times when a true supporting friend disagrees or says no, as was brought out earlier. However, there are also times when we must "let go" and trust that the other person knows what she needs. It is easy indeed, as well as very arrogant, for us to assume that a need we cannot meet or do not share is not a worthy need. Gail's concern for the elite group may be an immature one she will come to regret. She may, however, need to find that out for herself, the way I had to find out that I could not repair my own dishwasher—me insisting I could, a knowledgeable friend advising me otherwise. Sometimes, people have to make mistakes in order to learn they are mistakes! Mistakes can be a meaningful part of growth.

Life Phases. Someone who is new to a job, new to marriage or parenthood, or new to being a homeowner can have a lot of important sharing with others who also are new to such ventures. Indeed, people in the same boat can give to each other in a way that other people cannot give. However, it is true also that a person who has been through a phase on a given issue can be very helpful. The support may be in terms of some practical know-how. It also can be the support of being a "real, live example" that people can and do live through such phases! Someone who has never been in the situation can be helpful also. Sometimes it takes such a person to ask something so obviously relevant as, "Why do you do it that way?" When people are not in the same situation, there can still be an important match. The relevant match is on a shared understanding of the value and necessity of development and personal exploration, and the value of each individual's experience.

NECESSARY MATCHES:
EXPECTATIONS AND VALUE OF THE OTHER

Tit for Tat. There need not be a match on all factors. However, there must be a "meeting of minds" about expectations within the relationship and value of the other person. In most relationships, some kind of reciprocity is expected. That is, each expects to give something, and to get something in return. Problems arise when one person feels that the "contract" has not been honored and she is not getting a fair share in return. This may be because the expectations were not clear and shared. Millie and Mary had shared expectations for their tennis outings and valued each other in the setting of their match. Before they arrived at this "contract," accepting their limitations, neither was happy. The expectations are sometimes specific and straightforward: "Oh, good, if you help me with this job today, then I'll be able to help you tomorrow." Relationships may develop for the clearly stated reason of equal exchange, such as doing child care or carpooling. It may be understood, "this week at my house, next week at yours."

However, tit-for-tat expectations can go too far and inhibit the growth of nurture and of the relationship. Some people can be very rigid about "keeping the books balanced." They cannot accept the smallest gift without rushing to their pocketbooks or smothering you in grati-

Nurture

tude for a kind act that cannot be matched immediately. Some people have thanked me so much, I never want to do anything for them again! Others cannot relax enough to accept. They refuse even the smallest token of fondness and will not let other people listen to them in times of trouble. They are not comfortable showing their own humanness and need for support. They may not trust themselves or value what they can give, so they fear getting in debt and owing someone.

The Friendship Pool and Trust. A person who has "no debts" is probably living a very static life, with a very limited view of what life and friendships are all about. Lakes have a relatively constant level, but also times of high water and low water. The idea is to have a relative balance without stagnation. There are different forms of giving and receiving. Some water gets into a lake by tributary streams, some water by rain, and other water by underground springs. Some water is evaporated, some flows out. Without the continual output and input, the lake is stagnant and the life within dies. Thus, I speak of the friendship pool, or relationship bond, as more important than a highly specified tit-for-tat balance sheet. What is given and what is received need not be in the same form. With one friend, lending money is one of my inputs to the "total friendship pool." She gives to me from that pool, though not in the form of money. More generally, the exchange in friendships is assumed. "Sure, what are friends for!" is a statement that we have a relationship in which I expect you to ask me for help and I expect to be able to ask you for help. When somebody is thanked for helping or giving a listening ear, the reply often indicates that a return is expected or a previous gift is recognized and returned: "I know you would do the same for me," or "Well, you've helped me out a lot."

However, the more the relationship moves away from strict reciprocity, the more room there is for disagreement and miscommunication. As intangibles become more important, so too does a subjective weighting of value. Because of the subjectivity, each person must have an important trust of the other person. Only I can know how much I give up in talking with you about your problems. And only I can know how important it was to me for you to take time to listen to me or do an errand for me. I cannot know the cost you paid in meeting my needs, or the benefits you received from my gifts. There comes a point when trust and respect of the other person is an essential ingredient of working toward a suitable match and reciprocity. Along the way, each person can only be as clear as possible, with oneself and with the other person.

Thus, in many ways, the bottom line is that the most important and basic similarity or shared agreement necessary is a shared value of self and the other. Because they care, each contributes to the pool in her own way and receives from the pool in her own way. Each feels equal in the relationship. Thus, the lack of match in the form of inequality is the most serious hurdle in a relationship of meaning.

When Equality Is Called Into Question. It is very easy to state a position of equality and respect for other people as individuals. It is much more demanding and challenging to act in a way that really shows that. With bad habits, along with not thinking, or not knowing and loving ourselves, we can do things that indicate lack of equality and valuation. As relationships develop past limited tit-for-tat arrangements or sharing of some activities, acting as equals with mutual respect becomes more fuzzy. Problems can develop easily to lead to feelings of lack of the equality that is essential to deeper, lasting relationships.

Some forms of inequality seem trivial and superficial. However, they can be showing differences in basic valuing of each other as persons, or they can lead to one person's feeling that such is the case. When "dinner at my place" is not reciprocated, the issue is not necessarily one of concern about exchange of money or time. More often, it is a matter of one person feeling that who she is and what she has given are not appreciated and valued. For example, Lynn prides herself on the fact that many more people have entertained her in their homes than she has entertained in hers. She clearly thinks she is more important than other people. On the other hand, Sue is embarrassed about her cooking skills and her plywood furniture, so she looks for other ways to reciprocate and to communicate her value of the other person. Inequality can be shown in words as well. Lil is good at spotting other people's weaknesses and strengths. She offers her advice and views freely. There is a lot to learn from her. However, she arranges an imbalance: she can criticize and disagree, but the other person can only say yes, you're right. She too communicates that she is the important one, that only her views and preferences really matter. People who show inequality can still have a lot to offer. However, interacting with them puts some strong demands on the other person to be clear in making decisions. What are you willing to give for what you receive? Unequal relationships have high prices. Is what you receive sufficient to justify that price? This means that you have to know yourself. It means also that you have to value yourself if you are not to be pulled off center by other people's strong valuation of themselves. In giving and receiving, there is no substitute for self-knowledge, self-love, and personal sureness or self-anchoring. As discussed in the next chapter, women involved in activities with other women tend to focus on that.

CHAPTER 7

Women Supporting Women

More and more, women are discovering the warm rewards of nurturing and being nurtured by women. In spite of many pressures against women's relationships, women *can* respect and value each other.

WOMEN AS FRIENDS

SIMILARITIES AND PRESSURES

Women are alike in being women! This obvious fact sums up many facets of similarity that are important in developing bonds between women. Many experiences vary according to whether a person is a female or a male. Different self-views and views of reality develop so that a woman lives in a woman's world and a man in a man's world. It is somewhat of a wonder that women and men can communicate as well as they do. Certainly the sharing that is possible between women is strengthened by the background of similar experiences, including those specifically relevant to supportive sharing.

Sensitivity and Openness. Women are better than men at being able to tell what feelings are being expressed, such as those through facial expressions. Women's sensitivity to others is shown in their use of words as well.

Women's speech indicates politeness, warmth, sensitivity, and openness to differences of opinion. Men's speech indicates forcefulness, hardness and clarity, and closed-mindedness. The men's style is rewarded in the business world. However, the women's style enables more sharing and exchange of viewpoints. Also, women disclose more about themselves than men do, particularly about intimate topics and negative information. With greater willingness to share and a sensitivity to others, women should be better friends with each other than with men or than men are with each other.

Devaluation. Many forces continue to work to make it difficult for women to develop important relationships with other women. As discussed in Chapter 2, women are unlikely to encounter each other under conditions that encourage trust and valuing. Quite simply, women are not taken as seriously as men are, and the social world is not taken as seriously as is the work world. In addition, making the biological and legal family the focus of interpersonal concerns is an important cultural restriction against nurturing relationships between adults generally. Social activities between women are particularly looked down on or not taken seriously. Men's Friday night poker game or weekend golf has more cultural approval than the "hen party" or "ladies' social." The traditional "ladies' group" has been an auxiliary of a men's group. At work too, women are put down: "Those women are gossiping again." "Oh, keep 'em happy, it won't amount to anything."

When a Man Is Around. In mixed company, women get little chance to express themselves or to get to know each other. It is a very well documented fact that men dominate conversations. They interrupt women, speak more often, speak longer when they speak, and control the topic of conversation more than women do. Women also often compete with each other for the attention and

approval of men. Young women still report breaking a
date with a woman friend to make a last-minute date with
a man. Most women have had the experience of a man
entering the room while women are talking—the man
becoming the center of attention, and the whole tone of
the conversation changing. When a woman enters a room
where there are *men* talking, she is barely noticed,
unless she is physically interesting to them.

FEAR AND CONTROL

Relationships between women are controlled because
both women and men have a fear of bonds between
women, though the reasons may differ. Put-downs about
"the girls chitchatting" may be a disguised expression of
the fear. Some theories hold that men's fear springs from
the young boy's dependence on his mother and fear of
losing her love. Thus, without realizing it, men may be
very dependent on women and fear that a woman's
nurture will go to someone else. Whatever may be the
deeper reasons, men seem confused and perhaps threat-
ened by women getting together: "What do they see in
each other?" It may be that men do not understand how
women could possibly value each other.

Men's Displeasure. Women fear rejection or criticism
by men, and therefore sometimes avoid activities with
women in order to keep men who are important to them
comfortable and happy. The concern of men is one of the
chief reasons that women give for dropping out of wom-
en's support groups. The men sometimes are clear: "I
don't want *my woman* getting a bunch of those fancy
ideas." They are uncomfortable with women's exposure
to different ideas, especially the ideas of "mere women."
They may fear losing the authority to say "the way things
have to be."

The suspicions and concerns are not always vocalized
directly and clearly so that they can be discussed.

Cathy's husband invariably decided that it was time for the long-postponed family project when she had an important day planned with other women. And so she found herself involved that day in painting the spare room or cleaning out the basement because she saw no chance otherwise of sharing these activities with him. He controlled her by withholding his attention and energy and then timing his offers to force a choice: "them or me." Although most husbands do not do this kind of game playing, many do show their concern and confusion about women's relationships in more subtle ways that still communicate their message.

Control with Negative Labels. Women's relationships are controlled also because women fear that negative labels will be applied to them, with additional devaluation and possible rejection. The negative labels work as an extremely powerful control mechanism by which women surrender freedom. Many people seem to fear the label "feminist" as much as they fear communism or cancer. Often they fear because they do not understand the concept. What is not understood is feared or devalued. Sexual labels are often used to censure and control. At a simple level, a woman who refuses to break a date with another woman in order to go out with a man or who refuses a strange man's attentions when she is in a restaurant may be called a lesbian or a dyke. In fact, almost any kind of assertiveness by a woman or an expression of valuing another woman might lead to her being called a lesbian or a dyke. Some women participate directly in the name-calling. Many more participate indirectly by not trying to correct negative views of women. This does not mean that all women are expected to approve of the way of life of all other women. It means that as long as "dyke" is a dirty word, all women are dirty. As long as there is a clear set of negative labels for some women, then all women can be controlled by the fear that the label will be applied to them.

A Summary Example. Many of these points can be summed up in my experience with Jane. Jane was a married woman with three children, a high school education, a professor husband. I was single, had no children, and was a colleague of her husband. Our dissimilarities kept us from discovering each other for a while. When we later accidentally had a chance to talk, we found we had a great deal to share in spite of our differences. She talked of how she felt during pregnancy; I talked of how I felt writing a dissertation. She spoke of how taking a course made her want to teach; I spoke of how teaching courses made me want to be a student! She talked of how her husband came in tired from work and wanted only to watch television; I talked of feeling the same way. She told me how to clean my carpets; I repaired the lawn-mower her husband was always too tired to fix. However, as we came to see each other more than a couple of times a month, her husband became uncomfortable. "John just doesn't understand. He asks what we find to talk about so much!" His comments came to have sexual connotations that made Jane herself very confused. I miss the comfortable sharing we had.

SOCIAL AND PROFESSIONAL SUPPORT SYSTEMS

FORMAL AND INFORMAL SUPPORT SYSTEMS

Women are becoming more active in building formal and informal support systems of many different kinds. Women's groups have in common a strong focus on nurturing women and encouraging their growth. Thus, any person concerned with nurture can learn from these groups. There are groups for women philosophers and for women millionaires. The membership of some groups is "whoever shows up" at the gatherings. In those, women executives in state government mingle comfortably with women receiving welfare through that government. Some groups attract women who are about the same age. In others, seventy-year-old and twenty-year-old women exchange favorite stories. The theme of the group has tremendous variety. There may be exchange of ideas and information, plans for action, or "just meeting people." Some groups have a clear informational or instrumental focus, while others are more concerned with social and emotional needs. A group may have a formal name, or it might be referred to as a support group or a network.

Networks. The idea of networking among women has gained attention as one way for women to be helpful to one another by sharing information. For example, a woman might take part in a baby-sitting network or a gardening network. In the work world, men have long had support and access to information through "the old boys' club." Women were left out. How can you be an equal part of the team when the important decisions are made over lunch or at the poker table that are "for men only"? How can you have equal access to a job when a dozen men knew about it months before you did? Women's work networks—sometimes called "the old girls' club"—developed to help women workers have some of the advantages that men have had. The networks can be amazingly effective in shrinking the miles that separate women physically and in overcoming the miles that often separate women and men psychologically. A graduate student in my department called me for help because she had heard from a friend in California who knew of my interests from a woman visiting from the East Coast. Her major professor (a man) in a building next door had neglected to mention that I had expertise in the area of her research interests.

Sense of Community. For women in both the work world and the social world, networks help in avoiding feelings of loneliness and helplessness, by providing a structure, however informal, through which something can be done. They also provide a sense of belonging and comforting unity: "We're in this together." Within a network or support system, most women have a notion similar to that of a friendship pool (Chapter 6), with each woman contributing what she has whenever anyone has need of what she can give. In women's communities, as in others, some women are dominantly givers and have to beware the same temptations of overgiving that can tempt any woman. Others are takers, and would be called "on the move up" if they were men. Some women have times of special neediness; but they too can give when they become stronger. The women in the system strengthen each other by increasing the support pool of the community. The better the position the group is in, the better the position of each individual.

WOMEN WHO HAVE MORE THAN YOUTH

Women at the Top. Some women who have achieved, or merely survived, have a negative attitude toward other women: "I did it the hard way, let them do it that way too." They may make life unnecessarily hard for younger women. These women are called *Queen Bees.* I use the term *Big Mama* for a helpful Queen Bee. She is willing to help other women if she gets credit for it and if the younger ones stay dependent upon her. These terms are as applicable in the social world as in the work world. A mother-in-law or grandmother or aunt may be a Queen Bee who has an uncaring attitude toward what a younger woman is experiencing in trying to be Chief Nurturer and Chief Executive in running a home. The Queen Bee may be a Big Mama who will help if she gets recognition and dependence.

Fortunately, the Queen Bee and Big Mama patterns are not typical. More often, the needs and abilities of older women mesh well with the needs and abilities of the younger women. A woman established in the work world or social world has a lot of know-how gained through painful learning. Suffering hurts less when a meaning is seen in it. Saving others that pain is one source of meaning. By sharing the know-how, the mature woman gains meaning and the younger woman can avoid the suffering or at least know she is not unusual.

More generally, the more mature women are looked to for having built up a store of common sense, perspective, and even wisdom. Meanwhile, the younger ones have the energy and enthusiasm to put into practice some of the ideas for their own personal advancement and for community good. Some of my younger friends amaze me delightfully with how far they will go to save me from being asked to join another committee, while being sure my advice is sought in ways more comfortable for me. I gain the good feeling of contributing to them, and they gain the good feeling of contributing to me. There are many ways of helping each other out.

Pressures on Older Women. While women of middle age and older can and do provide some stability and direction for others, they often feel confused and tired. They are expected to be role models or mentors for the younger women, but seldom have they had anyone themselves from whom to learn. It is somewhat like trying to be a teacher without ever having had one. Meanwhile, there is less energy to confront the continuing tasks of life. Older women sometimes have their hands full doing their own living and growing in life. Also, protective tactics which were once useful are hard to overcome. Many years ago, when I caught on that "the guys" were not going to invite me to join them for lunch, I developed a habit of coming in a bit later and working through lunch. That protective habit, which I no longer need, is now difficult to break. As much as I want to ask younger women colleagues to lunch, I have trouble with the habit. It could be that, while I'm writing about the importance of women nurturing women, I'm being seen as a Queen Bee!

THEMES OF CONCERN

Women who take part in women's activities are ordinary people, and thus are no more perfect than others. But they are likely to be fairly clear about working together to provide nurturing environments for themselves and for others. There are many lessons to be learned from them, and many more rich experiences to be gained from participation in women's activities.

Attending to the Positive. A clear goal is to emphasize the positive and to nurture it into greater growth. A small step forward is appreciated by women supporting women as much as by a parent supporting a child. The step may involve repairing a sagging cabinet door, or protesting a sexual joke or comment demeaning to women. When a mistake has been made, attention is focused on correcting it rather than on censuring it. Instead of, "Why on earth did you do such a stupid thing?" the response is, "Let's go over the details again and see what we can do." Similarly, attention is called to a woman's strength when she is feeling guilt, self-blame, or self-doubt.

Feelings Are Affirmed. Women's interactions are noted also for the affirmation of feelings. So often, otherwise, feelings are put down as trivial or as not justified. Responses are often those of talking *at* a person in a judgmental way instead of from the attitude of an active, sympathetic listener: "You shouldn't be angry." "You oughtn't be depressed." They amount to: "You have no right to be you." Women listen and share honestly.

Perhaps you are seeing unrealistically and can use help
on getting a different perspective. Nonetheless, here and
now, you feel what you are feeling and have a right to
that. When women support women, feelings of anger or
depression are not explained away or criticized, but are
discussed with concern for the total situation and for the
woman's strength. Women are attempting to acknowl-
edge the fact that they have feelings and that their
feelings are legitimate.

Anger and Assertiveness. Of special concern to women
is anger. The message of society has been that anger is
unfeminine and inappropriate in women. Yet women are
people too! In the ordinary course of life, anyone is likely
to have occasions of anger. Women may have more
reasons for anger than men, and one of them is that we
are told not to feel angry. For many women, discovering
their anger is a tremendous step in discovering and
affirming themselves: "I am a person too! I, too, feel
angry when someone mistreats me!" When anger is not
accepted and expressed, it goes underground and accu-
mulates. With the big store of anger that many women
have built up underground, they often seem to be unrealistically angry when that anger is tapped and allowed
expression. Angry responses, like any new ones, take a
while to master. There is a lot of lost time to make up for.
This seems a necessary step in correcting the past and
moving on to a growthful future.

Assertiveness is a related issue. The social pressures
against anger and aggression are part of the broader
message against any active stance by women, particularly in their own self-interest. Assertiveness is standing up
for your own rights without attempting to take away or to
intrude upon the rights of other people. In contrast,
aggression involves a violation of the rights of others.
And passivity is not standing up for your own rights. It is
not easy for women to come to look out for themselves

and develop assertive responses. For that and for many other challenges, we need the help of supportive others who assure us that we are in fact persons with human rights. We make ourselves less than adult human beings if we do not meet our responsibility for self-protection. We undermine our ability to give to others if we refuse to be assertive and to take care of ourselves. Women must help each other to understand that.

Power or Equality. In women's groups, emphasis is on equality and mutuality rather than on power or a hierarchy of control. If a group leader is needed, the leadership changes from session to session or even from task to task, so that one person is not elevated in status and others lowered. One person may be able to cut through red tape in the bureaucracy, another may have some office supplies or some free time, while another may make an important contribution by having a house large enough for the meetings! The contributions of all are valued, so all are of something like equal status. All give and all receive. All grow. The power is in the group, not in special persons in the group. Thus, the women's approach has been symbolized as a circle, while other approaches are like a ladder or a pyramid, some people being on a higher rung than others, and giving orders to those below.

Trust. By far the most important aspect of successful women's groups is the development of trust of one's self and of other women, a sense of sisterhood or solidarity with other women as valued human beings. Other women become sisters instead of threatening enemies. As a result of participation, women who thought they knew themselves and valued themselves and other women report a new understanding. Often there is first a fear, and some women drop out early. Women have a long history of being taught not to value other women or to trust them, because they are, after all, "only women" and competitors after men's attention and approval. One way that women have been "kept in their place" is by keeping them apart from and divided from one another. The trust and solidarity that develops among women contributes to the fear and suspicion of women's activities.

The development of trust is aided by the other aspects of the interactions, including the emphasis on the positive, sharing of feelings, and equality. In the supportive context, one's self becomes more known, trusted, and valued because it is one's own and because other people whom one trusts say that that is so. Human beings need the support of others. In women's activities, women receive that support from similar and trustworthy others. They learn that they are people. They may want the approval of a specific other person who is a man, but they become less and less dependent on "people out there saying I'm okay—I am I."

In sum, the goal of women's groups is the growth of each person as an individual. Women assume that they can do that better together than apart. They seek nurture from supportive others, and seek to give nurture to those who accept and value it. This nurturing-sharing with other adult women can enliven and enrich so that nurture toward any person is improved. The affirmation and nurture of others is associated with affirmation and nurture of self.

CHAPTER 8

In Perspective:
Be Your Own Best Friend

Nurture goes to the heart of some basic facts about human nature. People need people. Together we are not alone. We have responsibilities to others, and rights about what we can expect. With nurture, we all can grow to be more healthy and effective human beings. Yet it is also true that each person is separate and apart from others—a solitary individual alone in the world, in a sense. "The woman in your life is you," according to a song popular among women. And, as noted previously, "You are the only person who will never leave you." We must be able to be our own best friend and to nurture ourselves. Curiously, the more we can do that, the better we can relate to other people and give to them. When we relate to others and care for them, we are opening ourselves up to hurt. Who is to soothe the wounds of care? We must be prepared to do that for ourselves as well.

WHAT IS NURTURE?

Nurture is effective love by which we can be most meaningfully related to each other in growth as separate persons and as participants in the collective of human beings in the world. It is an attitude or stance toward other people and ourselves, and a process of interacting with people. It takes quite a while in adult growth for this attitude to mature at really deep levels. Nurture is a lifetime adventure. Ultimately, mature and effective nurture is a way of living life, of being you. As this, it is a potentiality any person has. If it is to grow, the potentiality to nurture must itself be nurtured, developed, and fostered. Nurturing requires love and knowledge, of oneself and of others.

Your own way of summing up nurture will be most important to you. Some of the principles I see are:

1. Know yourself. Know what you can give and what you want to receive. Value yourself, your gifts, your needs, and your feelings. With self-love and self-knowledge, you can trust yourself enough to share honestly and to listen with understanding, warmth, and encouragement.

2. Speak to the strength and beauty of people—see with love. You are not really free to see another with love if you do not see yourself with love. Respect the other person's rights and preference, and, equally, respect your own.

3. To put these principles into meaningful action, obviously you must focus on yourself and be committed to continual personal growth in building from your strengths and minimizing your weaknesses. You must assume responsibility for yourself and your behavior, and be willing to accept hurt. This final chapter elaborates on this.

FOCUS ON SELF

NURTURING YOURSELF

To nurture others, you must nurture yourself. If you are not your own best friend, you are not free to be a friend of others. Other people can be helpful, to be sure. Do not ignore what they give to you. But you are the one with major responsibility for yourself and responsibility to yourself, to love and know yourself. Just as charity begins at home, so does nurture. Ordinary selfishness is not the biggest stumbling block in developing a nurturing attitude. Instead, it is not having real self-interest. Do you take yourself for granted? Can you pamper yourself as much as you pamper others? Are plans to spend an afternoon with yourself as important as plans to spend it with someone else? Do you know how to cheer yourself up as well as you know how to raise someone else's spirits? Being wisely extravagant and using first-aid kits can help lift the spirits or keep them from getting too low too often.

The Value of Extravagance. Extravagance can be a good investment. Women save up money or time in order to make a special gift to someone else. We need to do the same for ourselves. The extravagance is a reminder: "I, too, am a person of value." It can provide a pick-me-up, both before and after the fact. As a student with very little money, I treated myself on Saturdays to appetizers of deviled ham on crackers. My Thursday-night eggs tasted a bit better when I thought about the treat of the past Saturday and the coming Saturday. Today I do not often have deviled ham! However, I often wonder why I do not remember to give myself a similar treat now. The extravagance can be of time, such as lounging in a bubble bath instead of scrubbing the kitchen floor, going to bed in the middle of the day and reading a book whose only value is that you enjoy it. Exactly what you do is not as important as that you do it for you, as a treat. It is special to you.

The Child Within. The weights of adult responsibility often get heavy and make it hard to know what would make us feel good. It can be helpful to think of a child.

Most people can respond easily to the image of taking care of a sick child or giving a child a treat. There is a child within each grown-up, a child to be nurtured and delighted. Hug the child that is you. Ask yourself, "What does my little girl want?" Mine wants raspberries in February and popcorn in July. Sometimes she wants another cheap flannel shirt, or to do a jigsaw puzzle instead of grading exams. Although she cannot have all she wants, I find it easier to remember to take care of myself and to treat myself when I think of her than when I think of myself only as an adult who must deal with the demands of life.

First-Aid Kits. On some days there is no time or energy for the extravagance we should have given our little girls last week. You can always give yourself some contact comfort by hugging yourself. Taking care of yourself can be easier if you are ready for the emergencies of everyday living. Some people keep a psychological first-aid kit, just as they keep Band-Aids and aspirin. This might include a book you've been wanting to read or a list of favorite sayings that inspire you. My desk is surrounded by index cards with important statements on them that remind me of why I am doing what I do, and remind me that I can, in fact, do it! One friend keeps a list of meaningful compliments people have paid her and of the pats on the back she gives herself. A similar way of being ready for the low times is to write a letter to yourself. When you are in a calm, positive mood, write a letter to the frantic, fretful person you sometimes are. Take the role of a third party and be your own best friend. Can you be as sincere and specific in writing to yourself as you would to a good friend? To give yourself sincere, specific praise, you must pay attention to yourself and know what you value. Loving and knowing go together.

KNOWING THE POSITIVE AND THE NEGATIVE

Really knowing who you are is necessary for growing and for giving. In turn, the more you give and grow, the more you know yourself. What are your basic styles of relating to people? To yourself? How comfortable are you and others with your typical patterns? Do careless habits, defenses, and the Glorious Image get in your way? Honest self-appraisal is not always easy or pleasant. We all have some image to live up to and have defenses we have developed to protect us against some of the pain of seeing ourselves and feeling hurtful memories. Keeping a positive attitude is helpful in seeing through, or at least around, some of the walls of defense. This *can* be done without being unrealistic or too easy on yourself. Having the right attitude includes knowing that the positive and negative often go together, and that you are not stuck with the "bad you" you may think you see.

Two Sides of the Same Coin. Strengths and weaknesses often go together. There has to be some negative in order to have the positive—at least until we become perfect! I don't let a dirty kitchen floor get in the way when there is something more important to do (as there usually is!), such as writing this book, having a long conversation with a student who is having problems, or restoring harmony between my dog and cat. Am I just making excuses for my laziness? The same friends who criticize my tolerance for messiness can also have the comfort of knowing that, for me, nurturing them comes ahead of having an immaculate house—a routine of doing the dishes right after dinner will not keep me from attending to my friends when they call to be cheered up. I also have one friend who gets annoyed because I talk like a psychology professor. But she also seeks me out to ask questions about psychology. I need to learn how to

be neater and to talk less like a professor. But I can face
the hard work of making corrections better when I think
of the good that has gone along with the bad.

If you think positively, you can also see that a negative
feature can be changed into a positive one. A lot of
growth is a matter of learning to use what you have. My
mother used to tell me, "You're stubborn as a mule." She
did not mean it as a compliment! Now people tell me
much the same thing. But, more often than in the past,
they mean that once I decide on a course of action, I stick
to it to get something done. I am still stubborn, but now
in a better way. In fact, sometimes I am praised for
courage when, in my heart of hearts, I know I was just
being stubborn. (And, when I put my mind to it, I can be
very stubborn in cleaning the kitchen floor!)

Failing in Nurture. People do fail. No matter how hard
we try, we are likely to make mistakes. People who do
not see that they sometimes fail may not be really
engaged in life. Or they are unrealistic in their views of
themselves and of other people. Failures can be defen-
sively ignored or explained away as someone else's fault.
For example, Busybody Bumblebees blame others for
not appreciating their help, Efficient Robots or Fulfilled
Tape Recorders blame others for not being rational or
fulfilled, and Aloof Cynics criticize others for not helping
themselves. Yet blaming others does little good in our
own growth. It takes strength to see and to admit to
imperfections. If, besides, you can see what you did
wrong, you are in a better position to make corrections.

When It's Not All Your Fault. Accepting blame and
growing with that does not mean you have to assume
total responsibility. It is one thing to accept responsibility for your own actions. It is another to accept responsibility for everyone else's actions as well. You are not
responsible for the world. Accept that. You lost your
temper, you said something sarcastic, you were so caught

up in your own needs that you forgot someone else, or you were just too lazy to go out on a rainy Saturday afternoon. Why did you do that? Yes, you are imperfect. But what went on in this specific situation? Do not simply conclude: "I'm a schmuck." Criticism, like praise, is more helpful when it is specific.

Being specific and having a helpful attitude often means considering the total situation. Be as fair to yourself as you are to other people. You would help a friend to see in perspective. Do the same for yourself. If someone else were involved, you might say something like, "But look at the pickle you were in, no wonder you got flustered or lost your cool." Or: "That was a hasty action, but look at the bind she put you in." "How were you to know what was going on? She didn't give you the whole story." "Well, that was not what she needed to hear from you then, but you didn't have time to stop and think it all out." This way, you do not give your blowup or oversight or inappropriate comment a positive label instead of a negative one. But you do consider it in the light of the situation. People do not respond in a vacuum. They respond to other people's behavior as well as in the light of their own circumstances. Any one person's actions are influenced by the actions of others. The other person has responsibility too.

You Are All You Control. Although other people have responsibilities, you cannot change another person's behavior or attitude. You can change your own. "It is *not* all my fault, but I *am* responsible for *my* thoughts and *my* actions." What do you choose to do to correct the situation? In one case, you might choose to work on your 10 percent of the problem while the other person ignores their 90 percent. In another case, you might elect to end the relationship rather than work on your 50-percent share with that particular person. Even if you choose to end the relationship, there is something you can learn from it about yourself and about people. There is something you can do better. You do have responsibility for your own growth as a person.

Developmental Tasks. Faults can be better overcome if we look to the future rather than to the past. That is, our attention is upon the job of growing we have before us rather than upon a past we cannot change. It is a way of emphasizing the positive without excusing ourselves for the negative. Responsibility is not denied for the imperfections of the past and the present. Responsibility is assumed for improving. It might involve a general goal of being more patient, or something more specific such as writing thank-you notes. Focusing on the learning to be done in the growth ahead makes it easier to see something positive and to avoid feeling helpless. To be making steady progress is a high enough ambition. Thus, the realistic goal is growth—movement toward a goal. This more realistic view of life is helpful also during times of hurt.

WHEN IT HURTS

CARE AND PAIN

Nurture can bring pain as well as joy. When all is said and done, there are times when it hurts. No matter how hard you try, things do not always go right. You might get angry, but that is a disguise or a defense against hurt. People who are not much more than acquaintances can be the source of surprising anger and hurt. A gesture you made is refused, or one that could have been made to you is not. Other people seem unkind or uncaring. It is wise to pay careful attention to those surprising hurts. They can be showing motives and expectations we did not realize we have. A strong reaction is likely to mean that someone has stepped on a sore spot that we need to understand.

Yet those who hurt us most deeply are those with whom we most want nurture. Otherwise they would not have the power to cause deep pain: "After all we've shared, how can she do that to me?" "I thought I could trust you." "I have given and given, and you give me nothing." The energy runs low. "He never thinks of me." "How much more can I take?" "How could you think I'd do that?" "I thought you cared for me." By caring, you open yourself to being hurt. The only way to avoid being hurt is to not care. If you want to save someone from a burning building, chances are that you will get some burns. As Abraham Maslow said, if you cut yourself off from the hell within, you also cut yourself off from the heaven within.

The pain may involve confusion about injustice, with feelings of being used and abused, refused and accused. "It's just not fair!" You thought you could expect something in return and it does not come. What you have given is given to someone else, while you are neglected. You nurture a friend through a depression or crisis, and then the friend forgets you and, using the energy taken from you, has fun with other people. Sometimes the pain is that of seeing a loved one hurting or not growing. The suffering you feel for the person is hard enough. It is made worse by your feeling helpless: "There is nothing I can do." It is made worse also by your thinking you could help if you were allowed to, but your nurture has been refused: "Why won't you let me help?" This can be followed by the pained confusion of being accused of not helping!

It is always wise to check and recheck your motives and goals. There is always some more learning you can do. Were your expectations clear and realistic? Are you a martyr who likes to suffer? Were you honest with yourself and with the other person? Did you do the best job you could in showing your care? However, there are limits to the value of trying to understand yourself or the other. Sometimes the lesson is to let go, let it be.

LET IT BE

Don't Try to Push the River. There comes a point when you have done all you can. Perhaps there is more you could do, but you do not know what. Perhaps there is more you can do in the future, but not now. Then stop. Do not stop caring, but stop worrying, stop trying to figure out what went wrong. Maybe nothing went wrong. Maybe all is as it should be, though not what you wanted or expected. Let it be. There is a saying in Eastern, Taoistic religion, "You can't push the river." Have you ever tried to push a river? Or even a small stream? Yet many of us attempt to push the river of our own growth or of the growth of our loved ones. We try to push the river of life. We are impatient with the flow, wanting it to go faster, or we want a different direction. Similarly, Western religious leaders advise, "Let go and let God." Give up the worry and know that God will bring good results from a bad situation. People who try to accept this advice and face the challenge of giving a relationship to God can have a rude awakening about human desires and attempts to control life—people who think they are humble can feel: "But if I give it to God, God might not give it back to me, and I want it."

Let Go and Hurt. Where does one go with the hurt and pain? To pretend that there is no pain is likely to bring more problems. Another's support can do wonders. Yet ultimately we have to feel the pain alone: "The woman in your life is you." "You are the only person who will never leave you." You are not free to nurture others unless you are willing to feel the hurt that can come and are willing to experience that hurt in yourself and by yourself. Being willing to give and to accept hurt requires trust—trust in yourself and in the river.

People have a lot of strength. Sometimes we do not see this until we are up against the wall of the last resort. One of Robert Schuller's slogans is: "Tough times never last, but tough people do." In the last analysis, there is no substitute for a strong faith—faith that the river will flow as it is supposed to flow. People who believe in a personal God can have the support of knowing that God cares and God knows it hurts.

GENERAL REFERENCES
AND ADDITIONAL READING

Bernard, Jessie. *The Female World*. Free Press, 1981.

Block, Joel D. *Friendship: How to Give It, How to Get It*. Macmillan Publishing Co., 1980.

Donelson, Elaine, and Gullahorn, Jeanne E., eds. *Women: A Psychological Perspective*. John Wiley & Sons, 1977.

Fromm, Erich. *The Art of Loving*. Harper & Brothers, 1956.

———. *Man for Himself: An Inquiry Into the Psychology of Ethics*. Rinehart & Co., 1947; Fawcett Books, 1978.

———. *The Sane Society*. Rinehart & Co., 1955; Fawcett Books, 1977.

Harrison, Beverly Wildung. "The Power of Anger in the Work of Love: Christian Ethics for Women and Other Strangers," *Union Seminary Quarterly Review*, Vol. 36 Supplementary (1981), pp. 41–57.

Horney, Karen. *Feminine Psychology*. W. W. Norton & Co., 1967.

———. *The Neurotic Personality of Our Time*. W. W. Norton & Co., 1937.

Lewis, C. S. *The Four Loves*. Harcourt, Brace and Co., 1960.

Maslow, Abraham H. *The Farther Reaches of Human Nature*. Penguin Books, 1976.

White, Jerry, and White, Mary. *Friends & Friendship: The Secrets of Drawing Closer.* Navpress, 1982.

Whitehead, Evelyn Eaton, and Whitehead, James D. *Christian Life Patterns.* Doubleday & Co., Image Books, 1979.

158.2
D   Donelson.
           Nurture.

158.2
D   Donelson.

           Nurture.

DATE	ISSUED TO
✓ MAY 1 7 1987	Jean Kabun 676-4157
6/10/07	Rachel Day (989) 773-9578

FISCHBACH LIBRARY
PEOPLES CHURCH
EAST LANSING, MICHIGAN

DEMCO